BILL HALEY
King of Rock'n'Roll

James F. Cullinan

Pictures, period articles, etc., courtesy of
the John Firminger archive

April 29 1968, John Firminger at Chesterfield, along
with others, performed free on the same show as
Haley's, so that forever after they could say 'I was Bill
Haley's support act!' Meeting the singer, he found
him to be the warm courteous gentleman so many
others encountered.

Dig rock'n'roll? Then you should see the Finbarr catalogue
of books, CDs and DVDs, featuring many titles you will
positively not find elsewhere. Write: Finbarr, Folkestone,
CT20 2QQ, England (address complete)
or e-mail: finbarrrock@ntlworld.com

ISBN: 978-0-952950080

Introduction

Chris Gardner in *Now Dig This* (252, 3/04) wrote of Bill Haley relaxing with friends Hugh McCallum and Patrick Malynn at the end of his 1969 UK tour. It was at Malynn's flat (Sunday, August 17) that the somewhat intoxicated pair asked him if he would put on a show for them. He said he would if each coughed up his shilling (5p) fee. 'We'd have to see if the show's worth it first', came the cheeky reply; thereupon, strumming guitar, he proceeded to try and prove his worth. He gave them a show they'd not forget! He sung a few country ballads, 'Cold, Cold Heart', etc., before breaking into a lightning guitar solo. What they were witnessing was Bill Haley, guitar virtuoso, which, typical of his reserve, he carefully concealed from the world. His 'audience' clapped in between sipping their scotches, whilst their entertainer continued with 'John Henry', 'That's How I Got To Memphis' and others. But he had a further surprise in store: if they could provide him with a small hard chair he'd treat them to the kind of act he used to do back in the forties. This was a Haley fan's dream come true, for though all loved his rock'n'roll, it was the original 'hillbilly Haley' that most would have liked to have witnessed; but this had gone forever when The Saddlemen became The Comets. After briefly retiring to another room, Haley returned to ask his audience to imagine him decked out in a tasselled jacket and in cowboy boots sporting a ten-gallon hat. 'Good evening, everyone, my name's Bill Haley and I'm here to sing a few country songs for you', he said in a homely hillbilly tone. He bowed to his clapping audience and proceeded with a lengthy repertoire, giving a running commentary between numbers. The full panoply of hillbilly humour, built on years of entertaining families at fairs, social functions, picnics, and so on, was evident as he came out with corny gags and sometimes a hillbilly stutter. He sits on the hard chair and leaps up with a jolt, having sat on an imaginary tin-tack; belting through another instrumental he suddenly cuts it short with a thunderous plunk. Looking at the audience with an expression of embarrassment, he examines his left hand finger nails and pretends to tear off with teeth what transpires to be the supposed tin-tack! He spits it out, it actually being a piece of card, concealed earlier in his mouth. More tunes and gags, before Haley announces an 'interval'. This 'interval', he explained, was merely a device to sell his dollar 'Bill Haley Songbook Souvenir' to the audience, and which he would stretch as long as he could; autographing copies helped and sometimes he would wind up with a pocketful of dollar bills! Interval over, he continued the show.

Hugh McCallum was Haley's fan club secretary. That he could enjoy such a degree of camaraderie with the singer speaks much of Haley, whom Stuart Colman called 'that most amiable of men'. I am reminded of the 1979 video footage of Haley at the Birmingham Odeon: as usual, during 'Rock Around The Clock' there is a rush of Teds to the stage, promptly dealt with by the security personnel. As one is being strong-armed away he stretches his hand toward Haley who's just turning to walk away, having completed his act: Haley sees the outstretched hand from the corner of his eye and turns back hurriedly, just managing to grasp it for an instant. Whomever this Ted was, the magic of this moment must seared itself on his heart forever.

But I have not written this book because Bill Haley was a nice man. He was more complete than that. A much more interesting man than most of his contemporaries, he was also *closer to us*. Their music aside, there is little which we can relate to in our rock'n'roll heroes. They are outside the usual cycles of domesticity and routine which most mortals live with; how much easier to relate to the young Haley working twelve hours a day, supporting wife and family. He kept diaries and took a keen interest in every aspect of the music business. He read *Billboard* and *Cash Box*. He was focused, hard-working, conscientious: not qualities usually associated with rock'n'rollers, or pop stars in general for that matter, but qualities which are typical of everyman. So the fact that in the end he goes off the rails makes his story all the more poignant, not to say unfathomable.

It would not be an exaggeration to say that for most of his life he was not a happy man. We may trace the beginnings of this melancholy in the private tragedies that came simultaneously with his rise to stardom. Both he and his right hand man, Rudy Pompilii, suffered religious guilt and it is noteworthy that when the latter fell to cancer he believed it was divine retribution; Haley may have felt the same when diagnosed with a brain tumour, but it was not a death sentence though he chose to make it so. For all his amiability, Bill Haley was, alas, not an honourable man. I will not labour this point, the reader will make his own judgement as the narrative unfolds.

What makes him so fascinating are the huge contradictions and paradoxes. A shy, retiring man who could yet hold his own very confidently in public; a conservative and peaceable man who found himself at the forefront of controversial and violent phenomena; a man who love domesticity, but seemed always away from home. This is the same man who in the early 1950s had the imagination and foresight to set up his own publishing and production projects, yet became a factor in his later self-undoing. Having devoted himself to becoming a star, he then shuns the spotlight as much as he can. What baffles me is that given his first love – home and family – why, when already so successful and rich, he didn't organise his career accordingly, tending to his profitable publishing interests, performing only locally and perhaps going out on tour once a year. Instead, he persistently fell foul of the tax man, compelling yet longer spells from home, jeopardising the very thing he loved the most. He felt guilt about being successful; he may also have felt guilt about being happy. Despite the later clumsy handling of his career, he would become successful again and again. That is the other great enigma of his life: how his career never seemed what it appeared. He experiences spectacular success and spectacular decline. When he fails in one country, he is suddenly a hit in another. There would be inexplicable hits in differing world markets – there is not space to dwell more on this here – keeping him always in demand, whilst the perception in the UK and US was that he was washed up. An anachronism when he reappeared in the changed pop music order of mid-1960s' Europe, he confounded the pundits by his acclaim. 'Rock Around The Clock' became a hit again and again. This unassuming and unpretentious man was the antithesis of everything in the new pop music order, yet he rode high. He would have continued to ride high, but he had already sealed his fate.

I wrote this biography to satisfy my curiosity about the man – but he still remains an unknown quantity. Acutely aware of the limitations of selling to the R&R market (if you have a lot of money you want to lose fast, this is the market for you), I have tailored the product accordingly. The definitive account of Bill Haley's life and career has yet to be written. I only wish I could have given more space to the Comets – each one deserving his own biography. Fantastic musicians and a fabulous bunch of guys!

James F. Cullinan
Folkestone, August 2009

1. Beginnings

William John Clifton Haley was born in the Detroit suburb of Highland Park on 6 July, 1925. His father, Kentuckian William Haley, was a car mechanic. His mother Maude Green, a baker's daughter, emigrated with parents when in her teens from Ulverston, Cumbria. This was before the First World War. Young Bill had two sisters. In 1930 the Depression forced the Haley's to move east to Pennsylvania where they settled in the foothills of Boothwyn, near Chester. It was a musical family, father playing banjo and mother a classically trained pianist who taught piano and played organ at the Baptist church. Young Bill had already made his first guitar out of cardboard by the age of seven. His father, now making good money as a shipyard worker, would soon give him the real thing, as well as a bike. The boy was the envy of neighbourhood kids, whose parents were poorly paid farm workers. They recalled his good nature, letting everyone ride his bike; and he made himself even more popular by introducing ... cigarettes! 'His father had a cigarette-making machine', recalled one, 'and he'd get his father's tobacco and paper and he'd make cigarettes for us ... we'd smoke down at the creek, and that's how we liked Bill Haley!'

But the lad's self-confidence took a blow when, following a bungled operation on his inner ear, an optic nerve was severed, blinding him in the left eye. This left his eyes crooked, and he became very self-conscious and touchy, resulting in brawls with kids who poked fun at him. On his guitar he was able to make chords through trial and error. He learnt songs from the radio, possessing a remarkable ability to remember a lyric after only one hearing. He also taught himself how to yodel. His idols were yodellers Elton Britt and Gene Autry, 'King of the Singing Cowboys'. The local kids would sometimes organise shows at the firehouse to raise cash for their baseball teams, or some other cause. The bashful and reluctant Haley would be one of the performers, and these may be his first public performances: this would be about 1937/38. His first paid performances were probably at the local farmers' auction mart, held every weekend; colourful occasions where quacks and medicine men also hawked their snake oils and other dodgy remedies. Various entertainments were provided and the young Haley had a half-hour spot, appearing in a cowboy hat and boots. He was a popular act, and his fee increased from $2 to $5 per weekend. At first solo, he later hired Ray McCann, and occasionally accordionist Dot Davis, who recalls the ensemble playing, 'Has Anybody Seen My Gal?'

In 1942, at age 17, Haley was performing at various amusement parks around the states of Pennsylvania, Delaware and New Jersey, before being hired by Delaware hillbilly star Cousin Lee to play in his group. From radio station WDEL in Wilmington, Lee broadcasted a syndicated show featuring his group, which also went out on tour. It was on such a tour at Salem in New Jersey that Haley met his future wife, the beautiful, part-Indian, Dorothy Crowe (another account says they were 'childhood sweethearts'). Two interesting observations about Crowe's earliest recollections: he already had a kiss-curl when she met him; and he already had aspirations to stardom. The kiss-curl is not apparent from photos of the period, it being concealed by his cowboy hat. According to Marshall Lytle, the curl was there to distract attention from his blind left eye, it significantly being placed above his right. His talk about making the big time was not merely to impress a girlfriend; others who knew him at the time have the same recollection. When Haley joined Vogue recording act The Downliners in late 1944 after responding to an ad in the trade weekly *Billboard*, the group's leader Shorty Cook recalled his ambition to make records that would 'cross over', that is, records that would sell not only in the hillbilly field, but also in the much bigger, more lucrative, pop market. Most cowboy and hillbilly acts aspired to success in their own field and would be satisfied with that, realising there would be very little chance of crossing over into pop; so Haley's ambition was unusual, and surprised Cook who thought Haley the least likely of his crew to make it as a solo act. Though an excellent yodeller, he was otherwise perceived as unexceptional, this coupled with his one eye and bashfulness made him an improbable candidate for stardom in the cowboy and hillbilly field, let alone pop. Meanwhile he learnt bass fiddle with The Downliners, a popular hillbilly act in Indiana, broadcasting regularly from radio station WOWO in Fort Wayne. It was perhaps about this time that Haley entered, and won, the Indiana state yodelling contest. But in 1946, swayed it seems, by two other members of the group unhappy about the pay, he walked out on Cook at a moment's notice, the three thinking they could make a killing on their own. It was a bad move, for they soon fell out and Haley was reduced to busking and living a hobo's life riding freight trains, interspersed with gigs, billing himself with names like 'Yodelling Bill Haley', 'The Rambling, Yodelling Cowboy', 'Silver Yodelling Bill Haley'. He wound up in states as far away as Texas and Louisiana. According to Cook, a fraught Haley later came banging on his door in the middle of the night pleading to be taken back into The Downliners. Cook gave him the money to make his way home.

Though penniless, but perhaps subsidised by his father, Haley married Dorothy Crowe on 11 December, 1946, presumably out of necessity, for she was already pregnant with Sharyn Anne who was born six months later. The child gave him the inspiration for 'Rose Of My Heart', a song he later recorded. A son was born three years later. His activities at this time are vague, but we do know that he worked as a disc jockey, but could not keep a job with any one station because of his alleged tendency for playing black music when his remit was for hillbilly or pop. It is hard to imagine the seemingly pliant – and financially needy – young Haley risking dismissal over something like this, but it could account for his various moves of residence during this period. In any event, he found regular employment as a DJ at Chester's WPWA, a station which was to play a key role in his early career. Advertising itself as a 'family station' and notwithstanding the remarks of Haley authority, Chris Gardner, that it broadcast 'cosy shows' for 'cosy people in the Delaware Valley', its musical remit was varied, including a jazz spot that featured The Merry Men, a quartet that included Rudy Pompilii and Ralph Jones; moreover, it broadcast a regular programme of black music, 'Judge Rhythm's Court'. It transmitted to an audience within a hundred miles, taking in the metropolitan areas of not only Chester but also Philadelphia, Camden and Wilmington. November 1947, aged 22, Haley became the station's musical director, giving him control of all the entertainment. He formed the station's in-house group, Bill Haley and The Four Aces of Western Swing, which provided live entertainment with a show in the morning from 6.30 to 8.00 and another in the afternoon. But musical director or not, he seemed to be running the station single-handedly. He announced the programmes and read the news, as well as the commercials. He was playing hillbilly as well as black records at his discretion. He hosted a programme called 'Ladies' Aids'; he was even the station's record librarian and part-time janitor, opening the premises at 6.00 a.m.; this after a mere three or four hours' sleep following a night gigging or rehearsing with the Aces. Often there was no time to go home, sleeping either at the station or a fellow musician's home. This was six days a week, sometimes seven. Marshall Lytle, who would join Haley in 1951, recalls the Aces playing six nights a week at the Maltone Bar on Chester's 9th Street. Lytle knew their guitarist Tex King, who rented a room from his mother, and sometimes Haley would invite him and his brother, Cliff, to come on stage and sing a couple of songs. The other Aces (which was a quartet including Haley) were accordionist Al Constantine and bassist Bashful Barney Barnard. But the combo's line-up was in constant flux. King had apparently replaced Slim Allsman, but King soon left, replaced perhaps by Rusty Keefer, later to become a lyricist for Haley. Numerous others were cited as Aces at one time or another, including Cliff Lytle on rhythm guitar, Billy Williamson on steel guitar, Johnny Grande, accordionist.

Notwithstanding Haley's improved fortunes, his wife, a girl barely out of her teens and rearing a child, must have wondered if she had a husband at all. That she only had to turn on the radio to hear his voice, may not have been the reassurance she needed. But his career was on the move, though it would cost him his marriage. He had at last got a recording contract, signing with Cowboy Records in mid-1948. Cowboy, claimed owner Jack Howard, was the first record company to operate from Philadelphia, and was in business between 1945 and 1950. Howard, born in 1913, had a background in cinema which fuelled his interest in western so-called 'cowboy' music, he later becoming a publisher of such. He managed Hank Snow, bringing him from Canada: this was years before Snow became a big star. Haley had previously met Howard through Cousin Lee. Howard did not run Cowboy alone: he had an associate, if not a partner, in James Myers, who was a singer with his own group, Jimmy De Knight and The Knights of Rhythm. Myers also wrote and self-published: it was he who would later publish 'Rock

Around The Clock'. Cowboy Records showcased cowboy and western swing regularly from the local WCIL-TV 'Hayloft Hoedown' show – also networked by ABC – would also invariably appear on Haley's radio programmes. Artists would have to pay the 25 cents' production cost of each 78rpm record, whilst Howard, who didn't have a driver's licence, rode a bus with a box-full of records to dealers. Howard offered them an attractive deal: take copies of a record and pay only for those sold. Later he called back, charging 50 cents for the records sold (the dealer pricing the product at about 75 cents), and took back the unsold. Haley financed his own Cowboy sessions at the little WPWA studio; doubtless he also had to finance the attractive publicity photos and the sheet music. Haley in all pictures from this period is in full cowboy gear, topped by a ten gallon hat. The first record by Bill Haley and the Four Aces of Western Swing was CR1201, 'Four Leaf Clover Blues'/'Too Many Parties, Too Many Pals', and was reviewed in *Billboard* in the August 14 (1948) issue. The top side was co-written by Haley with Shorty Cook, a bright rhythmic ditty about a gambler's habit, featuring Barney Barnard on the chorus. The flip's vocal was taken by Tex King featuring a long monologue, in an excellent rendering of the doleful song later recorded by Luke the Drifter. Haley mailed promotional copies to other radio stations in the region, with a friendly 'from one DJ to another' note. The disc was also serviced to jukebox operators, and like other Cowboy releases, wound up on machines as far away as Chicago and St Louis. There was no income for either label or artists on jukebox sales, for there was an understanding that up to 5000 copies of a release would be supplied free of charge to operators. Why such an extraordinary arrangement? Jukebox operators were controlled by the mafia. So why did Cowboy, and others, bother? It was publicity; in any event, the artists bore the costs, as they did for every other aspect of their records. Records were seen primarily as a means of publicity and promotion for their shows, which was their main source of income. In the (unlikely) event of a record becoming a hit, an act's performing fee would rise accordingly. Total distribution of Haley's first record on Cowboy – and subsequent releases – probably didn't exceed 3000, with actual sales being less.

Haley seems to have had a thing about the name 'Jack'. His first son would bear the name; and early in 1949, perhaps feeling that 'Bill' was too plain and uninspiring, he toyed with the idea of changing his name to Jack. Maybe he liked the sound of 'Jack Howard', and that if he did change his name, he would have the same initials. Fortunately, he didn't pursue the idea, but he did modify his group's name to the Aces of Western Swing, dropping the 'Four' to avoid confusion with the new pop vocal group, The Four Aces. In any event, the label on Haley's second single made no mention of the group at all, his name appearing by itself. CR1202 was an ambitious release, for both sides were versions of songs that were currently on the national C&W charts, Cowboy aiming for a two-sided hit. It was reviewed in the 2 April 1949 issue of *Billboard*, the top side being 'Candy Kisses', a song already at No. 1 on a record by its composer George Morgan, who was not only coining it from his own version, but also from versions by Elton Britt, Red Foley, and Cowboy Copas, all of them making the Top Five! A fourth version by Eddie Kirk was heading towards the Top Ten when Haley's came out, which one would think was too late: but no, yet another version was out by Bud Hobbs, that was to rise into the Top 15 in May. Haley's rendering of 'Candy Kisses' was as good as any of the hit versions, whilst Tex King took the lead vocal on the flip side, 'Tennessee Border'. This song was also the flip of Foley's 'Candy Kisses' and itself also a Top Five hit.

Haley's version of the two hits will have been helped by WPWA's broadcasting of 'the first ever hillbilly and Western marathon' on 16 April, 1949. This was the singer's idea, for the purpose of raising cash for cancer research. Haley and the Aces went on the air for some 12 hours, inviting other local acts and dee jays from neighbouring stations to participate. The event attracted national attention and raised $16,000, a remarkable sum for the time. Bill Haley was making sure that his name got around. Yet, despite such exposure, neither side of the record took off; but that did not deter Cowboy from again trying to exploit an established act. Haley's third and final release on the label (C1701) was not even issued under his name, but by Reno Browne and The Buckaroos. Browne was a local TV cowgirl, and cowgirl of numerous 'B' film westerns. Although the vivacious blonde's picture appeared on the sheet music cover, she had absolutely nothing to do with the record. The label on the disc showed 'Bill Haley on vocal' in small print, whilst 'the Buckaroos' were in fact the Western Aces. The top side was 'My Little Girl From Nevada', a bright infectious ditty, whilst the flip, 'My Palomino And I' is a plodding sentimental ode to the cowboy's life and his horse. This is an absolutely charming record, and had it been released in the UK, it is the type one would have likely heard on Saturday morning children's radio alongside 'Four-Legged Friend' and 'The Runaway Train'. Despite the reservation of some, there must have been those in 1949 – apart from the singer himself – who thought Haley had what it takes to make the big time. But his next record was to come out under the name of Johnny Clifton & His String Band, utilising his middle names. It was a one-off on Center, 'Stand Up And Be Counted'/'Loveless Blues'. This may have been late '49, about which time Haley broke his hand. He occupied himself writing songs, and whilst he couldn't get a hit for himself, others would be successful with his material, such as Charlie Stone on Mercury and 'Pancake' Pete Newman on RCA. More changes were afoot: he disbanded the Aces and formed the Saddlemen, consisting of Billy Williamson on steel guitar, Johnny Grande on accordion, and Al Rex on bass fiddle. This unit was the forerunner of the Comets, and at the rowdy Luke's Musical Bar, a venue they played often, they shook hands on splitting performance fees equally. Apart from Haley, they had day time jobs, viewing the act as a source of extra income. Rex was amused at Haley's little basement office at the radio station's premises, hearing him declare that one day they would be big stars and would own their own publishing and record companies. They were an average hillbilly combo, not even professional; performing at ranch parties, picnics, social functions, Rex thought Haley was a fantasist. Cowboy Records meanwhile had gone into liquidation – heaven knows why, as the artists bore all the costs – yet on 24 January 1950, Haley signed a management contract with Jack Howard. Howard was to take 10% on a $200 gig; 15% on $201-300; and 25% on $301 or more. In April, Howard signed an exclusive agreement with booking agent Jolly Joyce, conditional on Joyce guaranteeing two dates a week. Howard's fee to Joyce was $150 per booking, $200 for a Sunday. Fees were higher for gigs over a hundred miles out. The arrangement worked and Joyce would remain Haley's booking agent into the '70s. Apart from his work at WPWA and with The Saddlemen, the indefatigable Haley also had a kiddie comedy act with Howard. Saturday afternoons, Philadelphia cinemas screened two westerns and a few cartoons, in between which Haley came out on stage strumming his guitar, only to be interrupted by the zany Howard.

1950 saw the release of three records by Bill Haley and The Saddlemen. Two came out in quick succession (January and March) on Keystone, probably a Jack Howard label, in view of Howard's cinema interest presumably named after the Keystone Cops: 'Deal Me A Hand (I Play The Game Anyway)' /'Ten Gallon Hat (With a Hole In The Crown' (5101) and 'Susan Van Duran'/'I'm Not To Blame' (5102). The third came out in December on Atlantic in New York, 'Why Do I Cry Over You?'/'I'm Gonna Dry Every Tear With A Kiss' (727), probably after having been released locally on Rainbow, a label which also recorded Danny Cedrone's Esquire Boys. Howard and Myers were probably behind these records and the John Clifton; certainly Myers claimed to have leased the Atlantic record and to have had a distribution deal for it. Myers may have also been behind a proposition put to Atlantic about this time: the label was enjoying an unprecedented hit with Ruth Brown's 'Teardrops From My Eyes' — #1 on the national R&B charts throughout the winter of 1950/51 — and could get a hit in the hillbilly market with a Haley cover. Though Haley recorded it, Atlantic weren't interested. Myers was one of the three key people in Haley's career at this time; the second was 'Lord' Jim Ferguson whom at WPWA broadcasted sports news and commentary. He had a reputation as a con man, yet Haley would later make him his manager which would ultimately cost him dear (beware of managers calling themselves by phoney titles, e.g. 'Lord', 'Colonel'!). Finally, there was Dave Miller (born David Kleiber), a local record manufacturer whose decisive effect on Haley's fortunes we shall now see.

2. Transition

It was 1951 and Bill Haley had introduced into his act a song which was to change his life forever. He had first heard 'Rock The Joint' when it was the signature tune for a WPWA two-hour programme for black listeners called 'Judge Rhythm's Court'. It was presented by one Jim Reeves who was white and immediately preceded Haley's 'Country Store' programme, inspiring him more every time he heard it. Whoever Reeves was – and definitely not the famous singer! – he was unwittingly one of those responsible for the rock'n'roll explosion of the mid-'50s! The record Reeves played was by Jimmy Preston and The Prestonians: it was rowdy and raucous, about as 'black' and marginalised as you could get – and about a thousand light years removed from the sweet cornball music of Haley and his ilk! Interestingly, it was also a local record by a local act, released on the Philadelphian Gotham label, becoming later in 1949 a national hit, reaching No. 11 on *Billboard*'s R&B chart. Preston was born in Chester and his manager and booking agent was … Jolly Joyce! Haley loved 'Rock The Joint' and in rehearsals with the Saddlemen he 'fooled around with it', trying to adapt a raw jump blues to a danceable hillbilly format. Then one night, 'more of a joke than anything else', Haley sprung it on his hillbilly audience, and was amazed at the reaction. So the song remained in the act, usually opening it, it getting the crowd dancing every time.

Yet, despite 'Rock The Joint', Haley was reluctant to commit an R&B number to wax. Dave Miller, the owner of Palda, a local record pressing plant, wanted a white act to cover a current black hit, 'Rocket 88' by Jackie Brenston & His Delta Cats, for his own Holiday label. Jack Howard and James Myers told him that Haley could be his best bet. Miller was a colourful but shady character, who didn't hesitate to use financial or sexual bribery – or whatever it took – to get his way. He had a police record. Haley was to wind up with a con man for a manager and now he was about to sign to a record label run by a crook. Miller wanted to steal Brenston's thunder with a rival version, which could only work if it was serviced to black stations as a 'black' record, Haley's white identity being concealed; whilst also looking for mileage in the hillbilly and pop markets, markets barred to Brenston. Myers and Miller met Haley and the Saddlemen in a bar, Miller emphasising that a 'black' vocal would have to be affected by the singer for his idea to work. Haley wasn't impressed, but the group were ready to give it a go. Haley, said Miller, was 'in no mood to record that fuckin' nigger music', a remark which may tell more about Miller than the singer, who professed to having dug black music since the forties. But this was one black tune Miller believed in: it wasn't the usual 12-bar blues, nor was the lyric the usual black preoccupation with women and booze: it was the celebration of a highly desirable car, bringing with it enormous appeal for white audiences. But Haley felt out of his depth: he was effectively being asked to make an R&B record, an almost unknown idea for a white artist in 1951. Unlike

'Rock The Joint' which he had made into a danceable hillbilly tune, he was now being asked to *be* R&B rather than adapting it to something else. Moreover, since he had failed covering a country hit ('Candy Kisses') how much less chance with R&B. In the end he was persuaded to take a chance, and so the song was cut at the WPWA studio, only to have it rejected by Miller for having 'the wrong feel' – obviously too white. Miller himself produced the version he wanted at the WVCM studio in Chester on June 14 at which time Brenston's record was No. 1 on the national R&B charts. The same session yielded the flip side of Holiday 105, a plodding country ballad, 'Tearstains On My Heart'. Compared to Brenston's, Haley's version seemed limp: for 1951, his vocal could be taken as 'black', but instrumentally, how the targeted audience could ever think this was not a white record, suggests a surprising naïveté on Miller's part. Al Rex's slapping bass, Johnny Grande's boogie piano and Danny Cedrone's hot guitar, certainly marked an aggressive development in the group's style: but their sound was still definitely hillbilly! And black dee jays would need no clearer proof of the act's colour than by turning the record over and hearing the Hank Williams-type flip! Yet the record became Haley's first hit, albeit regional – charting in Baltimore and Richmond. Needless to say, blacks weren't fooled and Haley was spared having to affect another black vocal for the follow-up, 'Greentree Boogie' (Holiday 108), a song he had written some years earlier, and which Miller already had out in August. This, the singer's ninth record, is the first 'immediately recognisable Bill Haley record'. It could have sat easily on a 1956 album or B side. It wasn't rock'n'roll but it was 'Bill Haley'. It became his second territorial hit, its flip being a fine self-penned country ballad, 'Deep Down In My Heart'. Clearly, Miller was good for Haley; doubtless the singer saw no money from the record's popularity, but he would have received both composing and publishing royalties on his own compositions, published by Haley-Howard Publishing. Through Miller, Haley was getting what he most badly needed: hit records, albeit regional; but he knew that regional hits could sometimes become national. His foot was on the ladder; he was getting more gigs, in addition to local radio and TV appearances (by this time he had ceased working for WPWA).

Miller was alert to covering more R&B hits and, come November, put Haley out on not one but two covers, back to back on Holiday 110, 'I'm Cryin''/'Pretty Baby'. The top side was a version of Memphis Slim's current hit and the flip was a rising hit for the Griffin Brothers with vocal by Margie Day, the Holiday version giving vocal credit to 'Loretta', who was Loretta Glendenning. Then, in December, Miller released a double-sided Christmas offering, 'A Year Ago This Christmas'/'Don't Want To Be Alone This Christmas' (Holiday 111), showing Haley at his most maudlin. His fifth and final release on Holiday was a version of Roy Acuff's 1938 hit 'Wabash Cannonball', more recently a hit for Ray Whitley under the title of 'Jukebox Cannonball' with modified lyric. This would be the third time Haley recorded a tune associated with Whitley ('Ten Gallon Hat' and 'Why Do I Cry Over You?' being the previous two), a cowboy singer and yodeller who had appeared in 60 westerns; and was a songwriter of some repute, having written a Gene Autry signature song, 'Back In The Saddle Again', and also designer of the famous Gibson SJ-200 guitar, country music's most popular design for some two decades. On Cowboy, he had three releases, but signing to Jack Howard's label was a sure sign of his career's decline. Howard evidently believed in 'Jukebox Cannonball', putting out no less than three versions in the early '50s on his Arcade label, including one by Rex Zario. Zario was an employee at Dave Miller's pressing plant, putting the labels on the records, and from such humble beginnings, he would later inherit Haley and Howard's publishing interests when they died. The flip of Holiday 113 was 'Sundown Boogie' which structurally and stylistically was identical to 'Green Tree Boogie'. This type of record, which I mentioned earlier as not being out of place in 1956, Haley described as 'blues inspired western swing boogie'.

In the meantime, Miller had formed a new label, Essex, a label that would prove very lucky for Haley whose records would now appear under this logo. His first release on the new label, and his thirteenth record, was 'Icy Heart'/'Rock This Joint' (Essex 303, March 1952). The top side, with its echo-laden plaintive vocal intro by Haley that immediately caught the listener's attention, was a country ballad clearly inspired by 'Cold, Cold Heart', so recently a smash hit in the country and pop fields, by Hank Williams and Tony Bennett respectively. The flip, in stark contrast, was at last the song that had been such a popular feature of his act, a song which in two years he had completely revamped, lyrically and stylistically, making it completely his own. Unlike 'Rocket 88', which was an inferior version of an original, 'Rock The Joint' was nothing like Preston's. If one hears both records for the first time, sandwiched between other records, one would think that they were completely unconnected. Indeed, if Haley had modified the song further and altered the title, e.g. 'Rock This House Tonight', he could have legitimately claimed authorship of a new song. Instead, it would be Jimmy Preston's writers and publishers who would cop a bundle from Haley's innovation. However, 'Icy Heart' was the side Haley wanted a hit from – and he got it. It was outselling everything he had done before: not just locally, it was hitting country charts as far away as Cleveland, Detroit and Nashville. Jack Howard, still the singer's manager, preceded him in a trip to their destinations, promoting the records and organising appearances. Haley was over the moon when he received an offer to appear on 'Grand Ole Opry' – the dream of every aspiring country act – but when in Nashville he received a call from Miller: sales of the record were surging, but it wasn't 'Icy Heart' people were asking for, they wanted 'Rock The Joint'. Doubtless some DJ – almost certainly in the East – flipped the record and got a tremendous response, rocking(!) Haley's agenda in the process. The singer was in a dilemma: he was a country artist just about to get the big break in his chosen field, for which he had striven for years, and suddenly he was in demand for an atypical country record, a record that just happened to be selling like hot cakes in not only the white non-C&W markets, but in the black too! 'Rock The Joint' was Top Five in Chicago:

Haley and the Saddlemen were booked into a residency at – of all places – a jazz club where they had to follow Dizzy Gillespie. Patrons were expecting a black act and when they were confronted by a bunch of country hicks in cowboy hats and clothes, they thought it was a joke! They wanted to see them perform 'Rock The Joint' and then walked out. Three nights of this and Haley quit. Despite the hit record, bookings continued to be a problem: Haley was a C&W act with an R&B and pop hit; black audiences didn't want to see a hillbilly act; theatres and clubs catering for white pop acts were similarly unsympathetic. We will return to how Haley dealt with this quandary. Unlike 'Rocket 88', 'Rock The Joint' was thought to be a black record: it had the feel, the energy, *the beat*. It definitely wasn't a pop record, but it was a pop hit: the vocal was rousing, the instrumentation hot and fiery. C&W records didn't have a solid backbeat, for drums did not belong to the genre. The Saddlemen didn't have drums, but Al Rex gave a hot beat with his relentless slap of the double bass. It was to Dave Miller's credit that he recognised the rousing effect of Rex's talent and placed a microphone against the double bass for maximum impact. Unlike 'Rocket 88', which the producer had to get Haley to record again, Miller loved the singer's arrangement and went for it. Rex would later claim he was the instigator of rock'n'roll: indisputably his slap bass was a key factor in the record's appeal. But it was Haley's arrangement of the R&B hit which lent it to Rex's gimmick. What Haley, Rex or Miller didn't know was that they had just recorded *the first true rock'n'roll record*. The record had attitude, push and rebellion. This was not an R&B record that could be labelled 'rock'n'roll': it was rock'n'roll *as in rock'n'roll*! It wasn't R&B and it wasn't C&W, but the offspring of both!

We don't know how much of a 'hit' 'Rock The Joint' was, for this was in the era before extensive charts, but Haley described it as 'a smash', citing sales of 400,000; but other sources suggest 75,000 or 150,000. For Haley, the record was undoubtedly a major breakthrough, but the figure he quoted is unlikely. If a pop Top 100 was published at the time – *Billboard* didn't start such a chart until late 1955 – sales of 75,000 may have got it into the 80s; 150,000 would have got it into the Top 50, suggesting sales and airplay in at least 25 states. Moreover sales in black stores would have got it into the national R&B Top 30. So far, our narrative is seen from Haley's point of view: but the Saddlemen were not merely his group, 'they were equal partners in the enterprise'. They were friends, not employer and employees, and decisions were made jointly. Haley was financially better off by virtue of his songwriting credits and his publishing partnership with Jack Howard, through which he had income from not only his own songs but also from the songs of others. The dilemma posed by the success of 'Rock The Joint' perplexed them all: they knew they were at some kind of crossroads, but didn't know which way to go. Jack Howard was a casualty of this situation, his place as manager being taken by Lord Jim Ferguson (the Howard-Haley publishing partnership was unaffected by this change). We may remark at the civilised egalitarian nature of the Saddlemen enterprise, for even the manager qualified as a member of the group, the income being split five ways. Ferguson's involvement at this stage was most fortuitous, for notwithstanding his dubious reputation, he showed imagination and resolve. First, he noticed that the fan mail which followed 'Rock The Joint' came almost entirely from thirteen to fifteen year olds. This would explain a lot: the people most keen on the record were the very people who could not see the act in beer joints and night clubs because they were under-age. Ferguson surmised that if the fans couldn't come to them, then they should go to the fans. The answer was to perform at high school assemblies: but there was a problem. There was no money in it: schools didn't pay fees. But Ferguson and Haley recognised they could learn a great deal from the experience: learn what the kids wanted, what they danced to, what they expected from a hip stage act. The group voted for the idea and Ferguson set up an intinerary of school dates, a development which would pave the way to Haley's biggest break yet. Then Ferguson marshalled an even bigger shake-up in the group's programme. Until 'Rock The Joint' the group had been confined to the clubs and beer joints of the hillbilly circuit. Ferguson changed this, securing summer residencies in the cafes of Wildwood and Atlantic City on the seashore. Moreover, he got the group booked into the lounges of Philadelphia which featured pop acts. Doubtless the group still did the occasional hillbilly gig; and it may have been about this time that Rudy Pompilii, another Chester native, first encountered them. Pompilii was part of a musical comedy act called Little Arnie and The Four Horsemen, playing to a near-empty house when he learnt that everyone was in another club further up the road where Haley was packing them in. He, a sophisticated jazz musician was amused by what he perceived as a bunch of country hicks; yet they were working up a storm. But Haley's hillbilly days were numbered. Whilst Pompilii was watching Haley, Haley would watch the Treniers, a black jump-jive act, in Wildwood, whose frenetic yet carefully orchestrated stage routine made a strong impression and got the young singer thinking.

Publicity photos published in the wake of 'Rock The Joint' described Haley's music as 'Country Jive'. There was a subtle but significant difference in the group's appearance: though still in cowboy hats, for the first time they wore regular shirts with ties, with Haley in a lounge jacket. But Ferguson was to take the change further for the new venues he negotiated: the hats had to go. It was tuxedos and ties from now on; even their modest sideburns were shorn off.

Haley was burying his cowboy persona. The hillbilly era was drawing to a close. But his group's name remained a problem. Bix Reickner, a songwriter and presenter of a jazz programme on WPWA suggested to him, 'With a name like Haley, your group should be called "the Comets".' (It was the English astronomer Edmund Halley whom, in 1705, discovered a particular comet, a star-like body with a long tail of light, thereafter called 'Halley's comet'.)

Other changes were afoot. About this time, bassist Al Rex left the group to form his own trio, thinking he could make some money (presumably he didn't like the idea of being out of pocket playing schools). His place was taken by

17-year old Marshall Lytle, probably less for his instrumental prowess – for he could not play bass – and more for his vocal talent, as Haley wanted singers for the act. Lytle had been on national TV, coming second in 'Paul Whiteman's Talent Show' singing Jimmy Dickens' 'I'm A Plain Old Country Boy' to Diahnne Carroll. This got him a regular 15 minute show on radio WVCH Chester. He had learnt guitar from Tex King and Haley taught him the bass, demonstrating the 'clicking' style he wanted. He hated it, for pulling the strings this way blistered his hand and only when he got calluses could he master it. Meanwhile, Haley's growing popularity was to have another consequence: Critics – all male – liked to harp on about his lack of sex appeal, but the reality is that women found him attractive. His unusual long moon-face, the curious but attractive kiss curl – surely a potent gimmick in 1952 – and his shy and engaging manner made him appealing and, to some, irresistible. According to his wife Dorothy, he had girls chasing him constantly, 'they just fell right at him and he was there'. One such girl was Barbara Joan Cupchack, nicknamed 'Cuppy', of whom Dorothy was aware. The marriage was already strained by Haley's long departures from home, but Cupchack was the last straw for the neglected wife. The marriage was subsequently dissolved without ill feeling. The singer must have been smitten with Cupchack, for he married her immediately, she presenting him with his first daughter, Joannie.

The last record out as Bill Haley and The Saddlemen was Essex 305 in June 1952. 'Rocking Chair On The Moon'/'Dance With A Dolly (With A Hole In Her Stocking)'. Artistically and commercially, this was a disappointment after the excitement of 'Rock The Joint', yet both sides are 'pure Haley' as we came to know it. 'Chair' was written by Haley with one Harry Broomall, an unremarkable song made entertaining by the imaginative arrangement and production. Haley's hoarse voice receives an echo on the word 'moon' and for the first time we are treated to Billy Williamson's exciting staccato use of his steel guitar. Haley was also hoarse on 'Dolly', a familiar tune based on 'Buffalo Gal'. This has a nursery rhyme quality which we may assume was well received, for the next record, the debut of Bill Haley and His Comets in November 1952, 'Stop Beating Around The Mulberry Bush' (Essex 310), was very similar. The song was co-written by Bud Reichner – he who had suggested the name 'Comets' – and the record was remarkable for the opening drum march – the first time the instrument had been used on a Haley session. With drummer Dick Richards' arrival, the act became a quintet, but he, like new bassist Lytle, would be a salaried employee, Haley limiting the partnership to the original trio and himself: a decision which would have later repercussions. The drum on 'Mulberry Bush' was purely for effect at the beginning and end of the record, the beat still being driven by the bass; but on the superior flip, the Haley-written 'Real Rock Drive', Richards is very much evident. Richards was also an excellent singer who previously had been one half of a lounge jazz drums-piano act, Richards & Lee (Stan Lee); and as a solo act had sometimes been backed by Rudy Pompilii and Ralph Jones, Jones being the drummer that himself would replace Richards later in the Comets (Richards incidentally was not Haley's first drummer: at least two others – Earl Famous and Charlie Higgler – had been employed by him, albeit briefly, for personal appearances).

Haley's preoccupation with nursery rhymes may be to do with the fact that he was the father of a five-year old; also he had a great deal of experience in entertaining children. He knew that such songs stick in the memory forever and he had the notion that, if adapted to hip lyrics for adolescents, he might get a hit. He had a point, for hearing his 'nursery rock' recordings over and over again they have an infectious – if annoying – effect. He was also preoccupied with gimmicks and novelty – whatever it took to get a record played or bought. Billy Williamson likened him to 'a scientist putting one thing after another through a test tube'. Every chance he had, he got the Comets into a studio to experiment, record, playback, analyse. He experimented with everything: pop, jazz, waltzes, blues – whatever: slow, fast, loud, soft. They studied Count Basie and sought to reproduce a brass sound with strings. Sound effects with guitars fascinated Haley and he constantly encouraged Cedrone and Williamson to innovate. The chemistry and timing of these two became an integral part of the new Comets sound, demonstrated ably in the busy and rhythmic 'Real Rock Drive'. This is a perfect record in every way, made entertaining not least by Haley's mastery of the 'good time' hipster's lyric: simple yet cleverly organised, saying everything and yet nothing.

We do not know how well the last two records performed commercially. 'Rocking Chair On The Moon' would have picked up considerable airplay as the follow-up to 'Rock The Joint'. Dave Miller had a 'network' of DJs in key stations in the East, jockeys which he 'looked after'. He would take Haley to meet them, the affable singer making common ground as an ex-DJ. So airplay for each Haley release was guaranteed, increasing the singer's publishing income; no wonder he was glad to be with Miller. But Miller was suddenly hot with another act, Don Howard, whose 'Oh Happy Day' (Essex 311) was hitting pop charts coast to coast at the end of 1952, eventually making the Top Five in *Cash Box's* national survey (in Britain, the song went Top Five for the Johnston Brothers). Haley and his Comets must have been impressed, and it was their turn next.

According to Johnny Grande, the act played 183 school assemblies, which we may date from September 1952 to May 1953. It is hard for us imagining school assembly being an occasion for a jive show, getting 'Rock The Joint' instead of 'Rock Of Ages'! Once, after performing at Marshall Lytle's old school, Eppington High, Haley asked the kids what they thought of their music. 'Crazy, man, crazy!', 'Real gone!' came the replies. Back in his apartment that afternoon, Haley wrote the song that would become his first smash hit.

'Crazy, Man, Crazy' employed every gimmick that Haley had perfected to this point. He combined two irresistible elements: the kids' jive jargon and the 'go! go! go!' football chant. Parents must have been alarmed particularly at the closing mayhem, the likes of which had never been heard on a 'white' record before.

Screaming with the group was Miller right alongside them, aided by his promo man D. Malasud, Essex distributor Garry Blaine, and the studio porter!

Coming out in April 1953, Haley's sixteenth record and his ninth for Miller, took off immediately, racing to the Top Three in Philadelphia and Pittsburgh, whilst breaking out in Cincinnati and Chicago. It was fortunate that Miller had just moved his Palda pressing plant, for he now had the capacity to press 20,000 discs a day, enabling him to meet the demand for 'Crazy, Man, Crazy' and the still popular 'Oh, Happy Day', in addition to his client labels' hits. That Miller could manufacture six million units a year, gives us the measure of his operation. Meanwhile, the popular Ralph Marterie brought out a rival version on Mercury, also attracting good airplay and sales. Interestingly, it was during 1953 that Rudy Pompilii joined Marterie's road band. Versions by Ted Heath and Oscar Rabin came out in Britain, but not Haley's, for Essex had no licensing arrangement here. By mid-June, 200,000 of Haley's record had been shipped and it was climbing the *Cash Box* national pop Top 50. National TV appearances beckoned, the partnership receiving fees it could previously only dream of. National magazine articles about Haley as some kind of 'overnight success' must have amused the singer, who had spent over a decade of working to get to this moment. The July 18 and July 25 *Cash Box* surveys showed 'Crazy, Man, Crazy' as the seventh most popular tune in the US. Bill Haley and his Comets had arrived! Personally, Haley was coining it in, for he was, unusually for the time, the sole composer of not only the top side of his record but also of its flip, generating income in its own right. Moreover, he had a share of the publishing income and also received royalties on the cover versions. Not surprisingly, it was at this time he bought his first Cadillac!

Despite the national attention, the act was committed to a six-month summer residence at the Broomall Cafe in Wildwood, where it packed in teenagers night after night. Haley recalled 'Crazy, Man, Crazy' as 'the teenagers' anthem', having the kids marching on the streets. For them, Haley's crew must have been the hippest act (the alternative: Bing Crosby, Vic Damone, Perry Como, Frank Sinatra, etc), for the flip side of their hit, 'What'cha Gonna Do' was one of their most exciting sides yet. The intro grabs attention immediately with their '1! 2!' shout followed by Haley's cry, 'One for the money! Two for the show! Three to get ready and here we go!' which the young Carl Perkins obviously dug. The side then belts along, propelled by the all-enveloping sound of Lytle's relentless slapped bass. Cedrone and Williamson are magical as always, whilst Richards is determined to make his presence felt with sharp, fancy flourishes and crashing cymbals all over the place. Grande treats us to a delicious honky tonk solo and Haley maintains the excitement with his rapid rhythmic suspended delivery. At this juncture there were two developments. Haley had befriended those other Wildwood regulars, The Treniers, and conscious of the endless financial possibilities in publishing, offered his compositon 'Rock-A-Beatin' Boogie'. Okeh, their record label, issued it in September. Whilst Haley had the

Treniers in mind, James Myers had a song of his own in mind for Haley. Myers, aged 34, had a songwriting partnership with Philadelphian Max C. Freedman, 60, producing material for hillbilly acts, secular and religious. Freedman's biggest success was writing the lyrics of 'Sioux City Sue', the top hillbilly song of 1946. Supposedly a 'songwriting partnership', in reality it was Freedman who wrote the songs. Writers entered such unequal arrangements because of the fierce competition of the market. About a year or so earlier (1952), Freedman had written a song entitled 'We're Gonna Rock Around The Clock Tonight'. Haley expert David Hirschberg (*Now Dig This*, 254) has proven conclusively, that Myers had absolutely nothing to do with the writing of this song, he having the cheek to place his pseudonym 'Knight' before his 'partner's' name on the credits. But it was probably his idea to re-title it '(We're Gonna) Rock Around The Clock' when he pitched it to Haley who loved the song straightaway, perhaps because of its resemblance to 'Rock The Joint' and another song he loved, Hank Williams' 'Move It On Over'. He introduced it into his act, at Wildwood audiences loved it, it becoming a highlight of the show. There was no doubt as to what was to be the follow-up to 'Crazy, Man, Crazy'!

Yet Miller wouldn't have it. Why? Because he was at enmity with Myers. Instead, he put out 'Pat-A-Cake'/'Fractured' (327), presumably in late August or early September. The top side, a Williamson-Haley composition, was a return to nursery rhyme territory and embraced the full panoply of Comets sound effects, bicycle bell, winding clock, etc, the singer trying to jive it up by emphasising, 'I'm gone, gone, gone', a derivative of the 'Go! go! go!' chorus of 'Crazy, Man, Crazy'. It's an entertaining side, but, frankly, a decided anti-climax after 'Crazy, Man, Crazy'. The other side, easily the better, a Haley-Lytle song, was also largely derivative, doubtless taking its cue from another hip kids' phrase, 'that music fractures me!'

About this time the act became a sextet. For the first time, on 'Live It Up', out in October, a sax could be heard on a Bill Haley record. No clearer proof was needed of Haley's break with his hillbilly past. It was the baritone sax of Tony Lance, who was also on the flip, the superb 'Farewell, So Long, Goodbye' (Essex 332). Both were Haley compositions and 'Farewell' did well around Philadelphia. Presumably Lance was only on sessions, for it was in November that tenor man Joey Ambrose (real name variously spelt D'Ambrosio and Di'Ambrosia) joined. Ambrose, a Philadelphian, was just eighteen years old when Haley hired him on the spot for $56 a week after auditioning him, he becoming a Comet on stage the very same night – without rehearsal! Though trained in jazz, the extroverted Ambrose wanted to do R&B and was allowed to shine in his new role. Every Sunday the group did a local DJ hop full of kids who went wild as Ambrose leapt and fell to his knees. One time Marshall Lytle, infected by the excitement, spontaneously augmented Ambrose's antics by lying on the floor and playing his bass overhead. Impressed by the wild audience reaction, Haley decided this should stay in the act. But just as Haley was finding his direction, Miller was about to become totally distracted. For in between Essex 332 and the next record, 340 'I'll Be True', Miller released British trumpet player Eddie Calvert's 'Oh, Mein Papa' (336) which exploded in popularity. 'I'll Be True', released in December, was a cover of Faye Adam's R&B smash: it is competent, but both Miller and Haley failed here, for the performance lacked the power and charisma of the original. The flip, 'Ten Little Indians' is as bad as one would expect from such a title. The Haley dichotomy would not go away: one minute he's the hippest act in town, the next he is singing nursery rhymes.

As 1954 opened, 'Oh Mein Papa' was the No. 1 record in America (and in Britain) and Haley must have been low on Miller's priorities. An air of desperation was setting in with the rapidity of Haley's releases and the inexplicable choice of material. When so recently the singer at last found the direction in which he should go, there was suddenly a creative impasse. And when he again raised the subject of 'Rock Around The Clock', Miller flew into a rage. Miller was betraying not only his act but also his own best interests by allowing personal animosity to cloud his judgement. Both Haley and Myers felt they were being robbed of their next big hit; but Myers was soon to devise a cunning revenge. Less than two months since the previous record, Miller released 'Chattanooga Choo-Choo'/ 'Straightjacket' (348). The top side was cut not in Chester or Philadelphia but in New York – and so probably was the next record – and has a slick, pop sound and a chorus more appropriate to Perry Como than Bill Haley. The flip couldn't have been more different, Chris Gardner describing it as 'one of the most extraordinary bad records ever made' – a statement unlikely to be challenged. The unoriginality of this instrumental and the guys' staggeringly monotonous and tuneless chant of the title, was probably created for the stage, and should never have been committed to wax, it being a showcase for the saxophonists' visual antics. The tenor man's solo spot would remain a permanent feature of the Comets act, Haley later substituting 'Straightjacket' for the more exciting 'Rudy's Rock'.

The fourteenth and final Miller release was probably the last straw for Haley, for 'Yes, Indeed' was not issued on Essex, but on a subsidiary, Transworld (718), signifying reduced status. Morale was further weakened by the flip, 'Real Rock Drive', being merely a reissue of a previous flip. 'Yes, Indeed' was the first attempt at affecting a black vocal since 'Rocket 88' and featured organ accompaniment. Bill Haley with a spiritual that barely rocked: what was the point of this? Meanwhile, Miller flew out to Europe, doubtless in connection with Eddie Calvert's follow-up and another Essex signing, the 101 Strings. His absence couldn't have come at a better time, for Haley and Myers knew that the singer's 3-year Essex contract was about to expire: that Miller was not more alert to this vital detail was another sign of his declining interest. Myers offered the singer a deal: if he could get him signed to a New York major – Haley's dream – he'd make sure that he would get to record 'Rock Around The Clock'; but on condition that he would thereafter record at least one Myers copyright for every release. This was a proposition not without its consequences, but Haley could hardly refuse.

3. Stardom

It is March 1954 and one of New York's biggest R&B labels has issued '13 Women' by veteran blues guitarist, Dickie Thompson. Thompson got the idea for the song after a chance finding of a novel with this title when clearing out his garden shed. The song's saucy lyric – which originally had no reference to a nuclear holocaust – attracted unwanted controversy and was dropped by radio stations. Its publisher, Dan Stone, turned to Milt Gabler, A&R chief and producer at Decca Records, with whom he had dealings over the previous decade. Gabler said he could get a Decca act to do it in exchange for $1000, and he would get the lyric cleaned up. One suspects that this was a private initiative, bypassing the company with the money going straight into Gabler's pocket! In any event, it would be the best spent money of Stone's life. The song would have been ideal for Louis Jordan – whom, as it happens, Haley greatly admired, but he had left Decca the previous year. Gabler's productions for Jordan had sold millions in the R&B market: he, unlike the usual majors' white producer, understood the black idiom. Moreover, he was hip to the newer, tougher R&B style and its growing legion of white devotees who could not be palmed off with diluted pop versions of the music. Similar to Sam Phillips later, he also recognised that a white act delivering a creditable version of R&B could open up a brand new market.

So when on April 1 James Myers walked in with Bill Haley he was more than interested. He signed the singer on the spot, the deal being for one year, subject to Decca's standard royalty of 5% on sales with an advance of $5000. The label would promote the act's releases through extensive advertising in *Billboard* and *Cash Box* and would mail 2000 copies each to radio stations across the country. (All very impressive: but remember, every cent a label spends on a production and promotion, including the $5000 advance, is deducted from the 5% royalty. So if the records don't sell, it is the artist who ends up paying the label, not the other way round!) April 12 was the date set for the historic first Decca session, the boys in the meantime rehearsing it at Haley's home. The two songs they had to do was the one Gabler gave them '13 Women' and 'Rock Around The Clock'. It is clear that the arrangement of 'Clock' that they would record was not the same as they had been performing on stage, and nor was it the same as the one recently recorded by Sonny Dae and His Knights. When Dave Miller refused Haley, Myers pitched the song to Jack Howard who recorded Dae on his Arcade label, a label in which Haley had a financial interest. Haley played them the Dae record, perhaps as an example of how the song should *not* be done. It needed more bounce so Ambrose, Cedrone and Williamson worked out staccato riffs on the spot. Lytle suggested Cedrone reprise his thrilling 'Rock The Joint' solo, and they changed Ambrose's solo on the record instrumental break to an ensemble of the sax player with lead and rhythm guitars with steel. Before we deal with the actual recording session –

which was almost a fiasco – we will comment on the studio and Milt Gabler's recording methods. The Pythian Temple on West 80th Street was formerly a ballroom, elegant building in art deco style, circular shaped with walnut-panelled walls, a high vaulted ceiling and a beautiful wooden floor. Decca turned it into a recording facility, calling it their 'Studio A', retaining the four foot high stage and behind it, or so it would seem, the balcony which Gabler had draped. The control booth adjoined, as well as a kitchen which acted as an echo chamber. The unusual acoustics of such a studio were clearly a factor in the bright bouncy sound of Haley's Decca recordings. In Milt Gabler, Haley could not have wished for a better or more sympathetic producer. Singer and band were comfortable with him as he guided them through the arrangements he prepared. He placed the Comets on the stage, giving them the feeling that they were in concert, thus energising them. Haley's weak vocal projection concerned him, so he placed him separately on the dance-floor at a distance of about eight feet from the stage. So Haley, facing the Comets, had his own mic whilst they had five mics between them, one mic being shared when they were a sextet. Rare studio photos of Haley at the mic showed him with sheet music, wearing glasses and without guitar. Drawing on his long experience of black rhythms, Gable hummed riffs to Johnny Grande who would make a chord on the piano for the others to follow, they working out their parts accordingly. Williamson would rehearse the group when Haley wasn't available. When the Comets' vocal shouts didn't seem strong enough on the playback, they would gather around a mic, with Haley closest, and record an overdub.

The difference between Gabler's and Miller's productions couldn't be more apparent. Gabler's were sharper and slicker: whilst Miller followed the time honoured hillbilly traditions of various instrumental solos, Gabler eliminated these and focussed on short and fiery performances. He was not interested in showcasing musicians' virtuosity but in creating records that grabbed and held the listener's attention. The 'lightning flashes' of Williamson's steel guitar, the sax outbursts, the thrilling drum rimshots, all these were carefully orchestrated by Gabler for maximum effect.

Milt Gabler was most impressed by the professionalism and dedication of the Haley crew, an impression he did not have on April 12. In point of fact there could not have been a less auspicious start, for he was on the point of firing them. The following is based on an account by John Van Hoelles and John Haley, the singer's son. Certain points are unclear, but at least we get the general picture. Haley was booked for 11.00 at the Pythian on that morning. He drives, accompanied by Grande, Williamson, Cedrone, Lytle, Ambrose and Ferguson (all in one car?); we then hear of a local ferry running aground on a low tide. Here is Haley, on the way to the most important recording session of his life and he is stuck on a 'muddy sand bar in the middle of the Delaware River'. Haley, not a religious man, beside himself, prays, promising 'the Good Lord something very personal' if he could get him out of this fix. It seems the Lord heard the singer's desperate plea, for the tide began rising and a local tug boat freed the ferry. Meanwhile in New York, Gabler was fuming. Drummer Billy Gussack was present, as was James Myers. Phone calls to Haley and Ferguson's homes in Chester went unanswered. 'Why don't the bastards at least call?' Gabler exclaimed, and turning to Myers: 'What kind of two-bit outfit have you been pushing me?' The embarrassed publisher tried to pacify him with his Havana cigars and an early lunch. Meanwhile, Gabler's office received a call from Haley: they 'will reach New York City at One'. Being sped through the streets of New York by a one-eyed driver could not have helped the passengers' nerves. Exhausted and hungry – for they hadn't had a bite since early morning – they scrambled to get set up in the studio: but Gabler didn't want to proceed. He was one of the top producers in America, for one of the world's biggest record companies, and an act to which he had offered the break of a lifetime not only could not show up on time, but were nearly three hours late. Haley and Ferguson pleaded; likewise Myers. At last Gabler relented, giving Haley notice that the session had to end at Five, no matter what. Ferguson went out to get coffee and sandwiches for the boys whilst they prepared for '13 Women'. They rehearsed the song from about 2.15 till 3.00, in between talking about 'Rock Around The Clock', Haley stressing to Gussack the 'lightning' snare drum rim shots he needed. When asked years later why Haley didn't use him as drummer for the session, Dick Richards explained that an unlikely combination of superstition and practicality influenced the singer. Gussack had played on his smash hit, 'Crazy, Man, Crazy' and he felt he would be lucky for him on 'Rock Around The Clock'; also Gussack was a far more experienced session drummer. Between 3.30-4.00 they recorded '13'; then followed half an hour listening to the playback, Gabler settling on take six for the master – relief at last for the producer, for he had his 'A' side in the can.

It was 4.30 and Myers must have been in a flap! If anything went wrong now 'Clock' would not get recorded, and he may have secretly feared Gabler presenting Haley with another song – one in which Gabler had a financial interest – for another session. All that could save the day was that the boys knew the song by heart and had perfected their arrangement. As his 'B' side, Gabler was not going to sweat on it. Take one was done, but on the playback all that could be heard was the band! Haley's voice was completely swamped. Time was up and one can imagine the state of nerves at this point! But having got this far, Gabler gave it one more shot, so used another tape to record a second take on which he switched off the Comets' mics, leaving only Haley's 'live'. It was 5.40 and Gabler called it quits. There were just two takes of 'Rock Around The Clock' on two different tapes and no time to hear playback. We don't know what happened, but doubtless the exhausted musicians repaired for drinks and a meal. The conversation would have been predictable, the guys elaborating on their earlier ordeal, Myers relating his efforts to save the day, and so on. One thing they would have agreed on was what a waste that 'Clock' had been relegated to the 'B' side, Haley doubtless adding 'We'll be lucky it comes out at all, let alone as "B" side! It got screwed up and we didn't even hear the playback! Either Milt saves it or we've had it!' They drove back that night, reaching home about midnight, Haley retired shattered – for he had slept little the night before – still anxious about what Gabler would do.

Gabler probably didn't lose much sleep over it, for he was happy with the 'A' side and with a little imagination could salvage the 'B'. So the next morning he took the first tape on which Haley's voice was lost – though the instrumentation was perfect – and dubbed it with the audible vocal on the second tape, synchronisation of both takes creating the master. Myers and Haley's relief must have been great. So it was May 6 or May 10 – accounts vary – less than two months from the singer's 29th birthday, that his twenty-second single, Decca 29124 'Thirteen Woman (And Only One Man In Town)'/'(We're Gonna) Rock Around The Clock', was released. Decca or one of its publishing associates, must have been recently the victim of some royalties' mix-up, hence the bracketed titles. Royalty collection agencies, when presented with similarly titled compositions, may distribute payments to the wrong publishers. It happened in the fifties and still happens today, despite modern technology. However, subsequent Haley releases would rarely carry bracketed titles.

Miller Gabler's faith in '13 Women' was well founded. Helped by full page ads in the trades, it quickly took off in several key pop markets and sold 75,000. Gabler, perhaps concerned that another major might grab a hot act on a one-year only deal, swiftly re-signed Haley, contracting him to five years. He wasted no time in getting a follow-up done and on June 7, in a much happier set of circumstances than those of April 12, he had the boys back in the studio for that hitherto rarity in the Haley universe: a consecutive great record.

The choice of material was inspired: a cover version of Big Joe Turner's hit 'Shake, Rattle And Roll', which had entered the charts in April and was to become the sixth top R&B record of 1954. But it didn't stand a chance of air play on pop stations on account of its lascivious lyric. So, just as he had cleaned up the lyric of Dickie Thompson's '13 Women', Gabler cleaned up Charles E. Calhoun's 'Shake, Rattle And Roll'. Criticism of Haley's version for its 'safe' lyric is founded on complete ignorance of the moral climate of the 1950s. Leaving the lyric the way it was would have doomed the record, which is perhaps what Haley's critics would have liked. With Gabler behind him, Haley was able to do with 'Shake, Rattle And Roll' what he had done with 'Rock The Joint': *make it completely his own and make it a rock'n'roll record, not R&B.* Whilst R&B and R&R were considered synonymous and interchangeable after the latter term came to describe a certain type of music in 1955, Haley had *already separated the two musics.* But neither he, nor anybody else, knew this in 1954. The trade categorised him as R&B, but he preferred to describe himself as 'pop' if for no other reason than he merely wanted to be popular, no matter what the market. In any event he had always wanted to be a pop act, but it was happening in a way he had never anticipated. The obligatory Myers copyright on the flip, 'ABC Boogie' is another song which gives Haley apologists a hard time, but it's saved by the singer's distinctive delivery and the Comets sound (with Panama Francis this time on drums), in particular Cedrone's wondrous solo; and who at this session could have possibly thought it would be his last? For, eleven days later, on June 18 he fell down a set of stairs, fatally breaking his neck.

Danny Cedrone was a New Yorker who moved to Philadelphia where he played with various hillbilly outfits. He was always only a 'studio' Comet, never being a formal member of the group. He in fact had his own group, the Esquire Boys which recorded locally and even had a release in England, 'Caravan'. A rare photo of Cedrone suggests that he was a thick-set man, sporting a thin moustache and a receding hairline. His face was round rather than long and he had a strong jaw. Haley was fortunate to have so gifted and imaginative a guitarist; but it is a tragic irony that he would never know he gained immortality through his thrilling solo on 'Rock Around The Clock', which was only an ignored 'B' side at the time of his death.

Decca 29204 was an immediate hit: in early July it was already hot in Philadelphia and New York and as far as Durham in the south and St Louis in the west. Haley could see that this was going to be his biggest hit since 'Crazy, Man, Crazy', but no-one could imagine that it would be even bigger and still on the charts the following spring. Inevitably, the record attracted controversy. Mid-August, *Cash Box* carried two interesting reports on the same page. In Louisville, where the record was No. 2, a local DJ explained his dilemma. The station management 'do not allow the play of this type of music, it deviates too much from the pop music field: but then listeners ask why the station was not playing "race-type" records'. Unlike his contemporaries, Haley – always interested in the business side of music – read the trade weeklies – but it is unlikely that the second report would have registered with him, for it was of no relevance: 'Sun Records of Memphis, have pacted Elvis Presley to a two-year recording contract. Presley is 19 years old and just finished high school. He has appeared at the Overton Park Shell country show in Memphis.' So appeared the first mention in a national medium of the century's most popular singer.

Whilst 'Shake, Rattle And Roll' was the climbing the charts, they were back at the Pythian Temple for their third Decca single on September 21. The gimmicky, if corny, bass voice on 'Dim, Dim The Lights' was provided by Dick Richards, but despite his presence Haley still had Gussack on drums. The session is significant for the debut of session guitarist, the wonderful Frank 'Franny' Beecher. Beecher was a jazz guitarist who idolised Charlie Christian and who had played in bands of no less import than Buddy Greco's and Benny Goodman's. After quitting Goodman's for lack of artistic expression, he returned to a day job in Philadelphia, performing evenings with a lounge act, The Larry Wayne Trio. Presumably because he needed the money he accepted Haley's offer of session work. In a scene straight out of Stan Freberg, whilst in rehearsal Beecher was playing an intricate minor-scale solo when after four bars Haley called a halt. 'Keep playing like that and we'll never sell any records'. Even so, writes musician and Haley biographer John Swenson: 'Beecher's playing on "Happy Baby" is remarkable. He phrased beautiful runs behind the vocal chorus in the intro, used augmented jazz chords as fills in the rhythm accompaniment and swung a breathtaking through-the-scale solo.' The tune was the obligatory Myers copyright, written by one Frank Pingatore.

Meanwhile Haley and his Comets were playing to packed houses wherever they went. We know from the trades that earlier in September they were at the Hof Brau in Wildwood (1-15) and at the Log Cabin (16-19) before going to New York for their recording date. Other dates reported include the Blue Mirror Club, Washington, October 18-24; the Gay Haven in Detroit, November 8 and the Casa Loma Ballroom, St Louis on the 17th. Yet Haley was still coming up against the same problem that he had after 'Rock The Joint', namely that he was presenting an exciting new music which some felt to be uncomfortably 'nigger'. Teenagers were buying the records, but it was the adults he had to please in the night clubs. Doubtless negroes also came to see his shows, as most of his appearances were in the north, but racism was endemic and universal. Haley's response was shrewd and innovative. Sell the act first, the new music second. Give excitement and entertainment. Soothe sceptics with pop tunes they know, ameliorating the R&B element with humour. Give them variety; get them dancing; and send them home feeling good. Repertoire and versatility were to underpin Haley's stage formula. New songs were constantly introduced, dropping those that didn't get maximum audience reaction. Dick Richards would come out from behind his drums – Ambrose taking his place – to take centre stage to sing 'Ol' Man River', which he would begin to render as a concert singer. The Comets wouldn't play, looking at one another shaking their heads, making faces suggesting they can't play such straight stuff. Then suddenly Richards would rock the tune and the Comets blasted in, the audience going wild as they built it up to a thrilling finish. Ambrose took solo with Red Prysock's frenetic 'Handclappin'' and 'Straightjacket', the latter now evolving into the future 'Rudy's Rock', which would also showcase Marshal Lytle's wild antics with his slap bass. Haley took slap bass when Lytle did his own vocal turn on numbers like 'Flip, Flop And Fly' – probably introduced into the act in March 1955 – and 'Rattle Shakin' Daddy', a number which the Jodimars would later record. Billy Williamson performed a comic routine with Haley and Richards as straight men; and then there was what Haley introduced as 'The Comets Trio' when Williamson, Lytle and Richards harmonised in their own spot, the guys practising while riding to gigs.

On November 6, 'Shake, Rattle And Roll' entered *Cash Box*'s national Top Ten where it would remain for ten weeks. The November 27 issue showed the record at its peak position of No. 5 and carried two reports about the record's controversy. Radio station WFAX of Falls Church, Virginia reported, 'Our policy now is that we do not play a record if it even sounds like R&B. This is a very firm policy, no matter who makes the record.' According to the other report, Haley had been a guest the previous week on Carl Reese's show on WERE of Cleveland, the singer remarking that, 'Opposition to R&B is unfounded. We use the familiar phrase here, "Nobody likes it but the people".'

What is so remarkable is that the record could go Top Five with so many radio stations – possibly 50% or even more – refusing to play it. The reason for the ban is self-evident: the record was alarmingly radical and subversive. 'Radical' for its rebellious tone and 'subversive' for its – to the ears of the majority – implied corruption of morals. Nothing like this had been heard on pop radio before: true, R&B records had occasionally crossed into the pop market, but none ever sounded like this. Too many people today have forgotten, or are ignorant of, the impact of Haley's record: nothing again could have such an unsettling effect, not Presley, nor any of the upheavals of the '60s and '70s, because those upheavals happened within a context that ameliorated their effect. No such amelioration attended 'Shake, Rattle And Roll': can you imagine hearing this for the first time sandwiched between Frank Sinatra, Rosemary Clooney and Perry Como? R&B records heard previously by the white majority were perceived as humorous, novel or merely entertaining: but 'Shake, Rattle And Roll' was shattering. It bewildered many: but kids were turning out in droves to buy it and it couldn't be stopped.

The radicalism was further emphasised by Haley and the Comets' appearance in Universal-International's 'Round-up of Rhythm', a film featuring pop acts such as the Crew Cuts. Filmed in Hollywood, they recorded abbreviated versions of 'Crazy, Man, Crazy', 'Shake, Rattle And Roll' and 'Straightjacket' – which included a rare boogie solo by Haley – in one day, and on the next, filmed over the soundtrack. The film is a relevation: a succession of crooners and lilting melodies, comfortable bland entertainment, and then at the end – pow! – Haley and his crew, hep, rockin' and crackling with excitement. As Haley authority David Hirshberg was to write: 'Viewing this film in its entirety makes one truly appreciate the revolutionary impact Bill Haley brought to the world of popular entertainment – sockin', rockin' excitement blowing away the pasteurised pop pap that had been the order of the day.' Even footage of the R&B acts of the day do not suggest a comparable excitement; and whilst much is made of Presley's earliest TV appearances, viewed alongside Haley, Haley has the edge. The Comets blasted out with a *charged* sound: Bill Haley was selling rock'n'roll, Presley sold sex. Haley provided the *context* for Presley's spectacular entry; Haley had no such context.

November 1954, Haley is riding high. With 'Shake, Rattle And Roll' yet in the Top Ten, Decca don't wait to release 'Dim, Dim The Lights (I Want Some Atmosphere)'/'Happy Baby' (29317) which hits straight away. But much to his annoyance, there is another Haley record out: capitalising on his ex-signing's success, Dave Miller released Essex 374, 'Sundown Boogie'/'Jukebox Cannonball'.

Meanwhile there were developments across the Atlantic. In September 'Rock Around The Clock' had been released in the UK (Brunswick 05317), someone having the sense to go with this side rather than the other. This was four months after its release in the US and it seems odd that Brunswick chose to make this Haley's European debut rather than 'Shake, Rattle And Roll', but this would have an unexpected consequence. British reviewers of the disc assumed that Haley and his crew were black, or 'coloured', as the phrase was then. 'Shake, Rattle And Roll' was already out in November (05338) and astonishingly – for the British public were even more square than the American and certainly had no idea of 'R&B' – entered the *New Musical Express* (*NME*) Top Twenty, appearing at No. 13 on December 13. And look at what company Haley was in: at No. 1 was pianist Winifred Attwell with her Christmas party tune, followed by operatic crooner David Whitfield and balladeer Ronnie Carroll at Nos. 2 and 3 respectively. At No. 4 was about as much rhythm as the British public could take, Rosemary Clooney's 'This Ole House', followed by the impeccable balladeering of Billy Eckstine. At No. 6 – Big Ben's Banjo Band! And further down, between Vera Lynn and 'I Can't Tell A Waltz From A Tango' by Alma Cogan': 'Shake, Rattle And Roll'!

The record passed the million sales mark, giving the boys their first gold record. 1954 had been their year, a year that had begun with disillusionment at Essex and ended with triumph on a major label. One can imagine the celebration and optimism on New Year's Eve: not only had they a smash in 'Shake, Rattle And Roll' – it had just returned to the No. 5 position, 'Dim, Dim The Lights' had risen to No. 15. They had become Decca's biggest selling act! Moreover, they were now hitting internationally, and to top it all, news was in that 'Rock Around The Clock' – the forgotten 'B' side in the States – was, months after its UK release, suddenly also about to enter the British Top 20! One can imagine Haley's pride and delight when giving this news to his English mother.

Both Haley records were effectively 'banned' by the BBC, record buyers first hearing them on the hugely influential Radio Luxembourg. As in the US, the assumed majority of purchasers were teenagers. There was another component, Teddy Boys. Originally known as 'Edwardians', because they dressed like Edwardian gentry, newspapers labelled them 'Teddy Boys' in about 1953. Most of them were nothing more than yobs, forming gangs which fought one another and intimidating anyone else., hence the news headlines. It was their appearance that set them apart, the basic attire consisting of drape jacket, waistcoat and drainpipe trousers, the style varying according to area and gang. Thick crepe-soled shoes and luminous socks became a universal feature as did the greasy quiffed hairstyle. The quiff was mandatory, but sideburns were not: some wore none, others sported fearsome 'burns which reached the jaw. Tattoos and piercings were optional. Teddy Boys were not particularly interested in music, as they were a new phenomenon they had not found an art form to identify with: there was a vacuum and the rebellious music of Bill Haley filled it. They were shunned by adults and the

Establishment, as was Haley, so as the saying goes, 'They were made for one another.' So, for the first time, a youth culture identified itself with a particular music – even a particular singer – an identification that underlined its rejection of authority. The music didn't yet have a name but it would be forever wedded to the Teddy Boy.

January 5, 1955: Decca's new golden boy was back in the studio for his fourth single for the label. The mood must have been euphoric, particularly that of Haley, Williamson and Grande, who were recording their own co-written song for both sides of the single. 'Mambo Rock' was an infectious exploit of the current Latin dance fad, with the emphasis more on the 'rock' than the 'mambo'; and its flip, 'Birth Of The Boogie' was as pure Haley rock'n'roll as you could get. Dick Richards was present for the tom tom whilst Gussack was the usual drummer.

January 8, Bill Haley and His Comets had two records simultaneously in the Top Twenty on both sides of the Atlantic. In the States, 'Shake, Rattle And Roll' was at No. 11 and 'Dim, Dim The Lights' at 15; in Britain, 'Shake, Rattle And Roll' had risen to No. 10 whilst 'Rock Around The Clock' entered at 17, but would rise no higher.

Then, January 10-16, Haley packed them in at Washington's Casino Royal, whilst on the 15th the press reported a nationwide car safety bumper sticker campaign sponsored by Decca Records and featuring the record, 'Dim, Dim The Lights' (nice one, considering the one-eyed singer's mad dash through the streets of New York at 90 miles an hour). January 22, 'Shake, Rattle And Roll' reaches its top position in the UK at No. 4 and 'Dim, Dim The Lights' peaks in the US at 11. Meanwhile, 'Rock Around The Clock' had been licensed from MGM for inclusion in the forthcoming Glenn Ford film, 'Blackboard Jungle'. Ford's son, Peter, was a hip 9-year-old who, like so many others, was tuning into the black radio stations and the music of The Clovers, Faye Adams, The Midnighters, and so on. He had bought both Haley's 'Crazy, Man, Crazy' and '13 Women'. When 'Blackboard Jungle' director Richard Brooks called at the Ford's home he heard the kid playing 'Rock Around The Clock'; he borrowed the record, thinking it could be useful. MGM subsequently paid Decca $5000 for the rights to use it not more than three times in the film. The young Ford recalls the thrill of hearing it for the first time in the cinema when the film received its premier at the Encino theatre in the San Fernando Valley on February 2. All his father could tell him was that 'his song' was 'somewhere in the movie'; but what neither expected was the record blasting out over the opening credits. The thrill of this moment never left the memory of the young Ford. According to a February 12 report in *Cash Box*, the film was to go on general release March 25.

Another development at this time was also to have a decisive effect on Haley's career. The hugely influential disc jockey Alan Freed, formerly of Cleveland, now of New York, relentlessly played R&B records although on a pop station, making him responsible for turning R&B hits into pop. More black records were finding their way on to the pop charts because white teenagers were asking for them in white stores. The kids loved the colourful Freed who on air would ring a cowbell and punch a phone directory to the beat of the music whilst yelling, 'Rock! Rock! Rock!', 'Let's go! Rock out!', 'Rock'n'roll!', and so on. These and other phrases were applied to the music, but were not its name. Though modern writers are at pains to emphasise the sexual innuendo implicit in such terms in old blues records, such terms also had a purely innocuous and playful meaning as used by Freed. The record trade, noting Freed's constant use of 'rock'n'roll', not surprisingly began calling R&B by this name as a good marketing gimmick. Freed realised he had unwittingly coined a new musical term and his thoughts of trademarking it were too late, for everyone in the trade was already using it. So at the beginning of 1955 when the term 'rock'n'roll' gained currency as the name of a particular music, that music was R&B. But what is 'rhythm and blues'? We first need to understand something which still baffles many Britons. 'Rhythm and blues' was a term adopted by the trade in the late 1940s to *identify a particular market*: that market being the negro (how unfashionable to use that term; but why not?) radio listener and record buyer, serviced by (usually) black-owned radio stations and record dealers. Markets were segregated, reflecting American society: blacks buying their records in their own neighbourhoods, whites in theirs. 'Black' equalled 'R&B', 'white' equalled 'pop', or 'Country and Western'. Roughly, the R&B market constituted 10% of all US sales and air play, 'pop' constituted 70% and C&W 15%. Still other markets, Latin, Hispanic and other ethnic groupings, accounted for another 5%. What particularly confuses some is the equation of the market with the music. Remember, that 'R&B' is first and foremost a marketing term. One can look at the R&B charts of the 1950s and wonder what on earth Andy Williams and the Chipmunks are doing in them. The answer is simple: *black people with access only to black record stores were asking for these acts.* Black record buyers didn't care if what they wanted wasn't blues or jazz, or whatever else blacks are supposed to like. Indeed black stores might also carry regular stocks of Hank Williams and Perry Como alongside Muddy Waters and Ray Charles!

In any event, the majority of records on the R&B charts were by black artists and were either of a 'rhythmic' or 'blues' nature. But the styles varied considerably: 'rhythmic' could be the jazzy Nat 'King' Cole and Dinah Washington or the teenage-favoured Dominoes and Drifters. Then there were the low down blues of the 'Woke up this morning and found myself dead' variety, and so on.

The remarkable Freed – a white man in his thirties, brought up on swing and also a lover of classical music, precisely the kind of man you'd expect to loathe the new teenagers' music – loved it and believed in it. The beat, the honkin' saxes, the idiosyncratic vocals – they all 'rocked and rolled' for Freed. And before he realised what had happened, the trade had adopted his phrase as a good marketing gimmick. The trade liked the new term, because it had 'crossover appeal' for the white market and was untainted by the colour implication of 'R&B'. 'R&B' would not be made redundant, however, because the segregation of markets would remain unchanged. Here is another point many misunderstand. Because the trade adopted the term, it would forever afterward be used as a marketing tool. Remember, the trade was operated by people who didn't give a hoot about the music – privately most hated it – its sole aim being to sell more records. Rock'n'roll to the trade now meant this: 'black inspired records that sold not only in the R&B field but also in pop, the buyers always being youngsters'. Freed, on the other hand, was not your typical industry man, for he actually loved the music. In the coming years he would see his 'rock'n'roll' mis-used and manipulated by the trade. The trade, for example, would see 'Long Tall Sally' by both Little Richard and Pat Boone as 'rock'n'roll', but to Freed, Boone's record was anathema. With the passage of time the trade forgot the 'black inspired' aspect and applied the term to anything that sold to teenagers, be it Fats Domino or Frankie Avalon – it was all the same rubbish to them.

Interestingly, the first to be called 'King of Rock'n'Roll' was Alan Freed; but Freed dug Haley from the outset. Meanwhile, the singer was having his first national breakthrough on the R&B charts with 'Dim, Dim The Lights' which reached No. 10 in February. As an R&B act, Haley would also be now called 'rock'n'roll', but what no-one realised, least of all Haley himself, is that he had already been performing R&R since 1952. The realisation came after the term was coined: R&R was going to take a form and identity of its own, independent of trade hype and of race. Within a year this would be manifest with Little Richard and Elvis Presley: these were not R&B acts who happened to be 'rockn'roll'. They were, like Haley, rock'n'roll pure and simple. And nowhere was this better understood than in Britain, where we were not hampered by any conception of 'R&B', and where it meant music with drive and a beat and an attitude, and lyrically always from a teenager's point of view. It would mean Lewis, Richard, Vincent, Cochran, Berry, and so on. It would *never* mean Boone, Anka, Avalon as in the US, let alone in later years the Beatles and co. America was its natural home, Britain its spiritual. American R&R acts through the decades have always been surprised by their reception in the UK, unlike the US where they were either unknown or forgotten.

February 1955. Even though 'Dim, Dim The Lights' – now passing the half-million sales' mark – and 'Shake, Rattle And Roll' are still in the Top 30, Decca release 'Mambo Rock' (29418) which becomes another immediate hit; moreover the kids are also going for the flip, 'Birth Of The Boogie'. Remarkably, by March 5, Haley has no less than four sides simultaneously in the American Top 50, with 'Shake, Rattle And Roll' appearing for the 32nd consecutive week, longer than any other record on the chart. Haley was strongest in sales, faring less well in radio airplay and jukebox plays, reflecting the white establishment's anxiety about his music. The trade journals reported the following personal appearances. February 5 in Rome, New York; in April at Brighampton, New York (14th); Boston

(15th); Baltimore (16th); Cleveland (17th); and Buffalo on the 18th. The act then returned to Rome on the 19th, followed by four nights in Plainville, Connecticut (20-23rd), before a gig in home territory at Wilmington on the 24th. Meanwhile on March 19, 'Mambo Rock' had peaked at No. 18 whilst the following week, 'Birth Of The Boogie' peaked at 26. This was Haley's first big two-sided hit and if the split sales were combined the disc was in point of fact as big as 'Shake, Rattle And Roll': it certainly was the act's most profitable, for they – or three of them – had written both sides. Amidst all this success, Haley was peeved to find that Dave Miller was again jumping on the bandwagon, this time with the reissue of 'Rocket 88' (Essex 381; flip, 'Greentree Boogie') which compared to his Decca records sounded crude.

'Mambo Rock' gave Haley his third UK hit when it entered the *NME* Top 20 at No. 14; but it would rise no higher.

Back in the States, there was no let up in Decca's promotion of Haley. Whilst the latest hit was yet in the Top 30, they hyped 'Rock Around The Clock' as the new single to capitalise on the national release of 'Blackboard Jungle'. The film was an immediate hit. Evan Hunter, author of the current best seller on which the film was based, was delighted with the inclusion of Haley's record, it giving the film a kick from the very beginning. He describes kids arriving at cinemas with copies of the book stuck in their jean back pockets, they dancing in the aisles to Haley's record. The film was controversial on a number of accounts. Its portrayal of vulnerable school teachers menaced by a class of hoodlums, emphasised by sharp and gloomy photography and an air of desperation and futility, disturbed many. Indeed, the film disturbs today. Yet it is credited with giving 'lonely and misunderstood teenagers an identity'. Actually it's hard to imagine such an audience identifying with the louts in the film. Most kids are more alienated by louts than teachers and the 'lonelier' they are the greater the alienation. The attraction of the film was more Haley's record than the ugliness of its characters. Here was the right record at the right time, hitting the right audience. What the teenage audience was actually responding to was the expression of boredom with school and the status quo, preferring to have fun all the time, conveyed in the idea of 'rock around the clock'. The film's violence was more incidental than integral, for most kids were never that way inclined. No greater misunderstanding of the R&R fan's attitude can be apparent than the pivotal scene of teacher Dadier's (Glen Ford) precious jazz 78 being smashed by a scumbag. One thing that all R&R fans have in common is their almost religious reverence for the recorded medium of their music; and as much as most may loathe jazz, the idea of deliberately breaking *any* record is unthinkable because the medium itself is the source of their own joy. Curiously, the only real life examples we have of such violence are of jazz and swing disc jockeys ceremoniously smashing R&R records on air, with station owners' full blessing.

Whilst 'Rock Around The Clock' was climbing the charts, on May 10 Haley was already in the studio for his next single. This was another two-sided gas, the top deck being 'Razzle Dazzle', from the pen of Charles E. Calhoun, writer of 'Shake, Rattle And Roll'. The flip, the obligatory Myers copyright, 'Two Hound Dogs', written by Haley and Frank Pingatore, Pingatore having previously written 'Happy Baby'. 'Hound Dogs' had a clever lyric, typical of Haley's knack of exploiting gimmicks and phrases, about two canines, one named 'Rhythm', the other 'Blues'. The side closes with the same mayhem as 'Crazy, Man, Crazy' – heaven knows what parents thought when they heard their kids listening to stuff like this! – with Dick Richards providing the final howl. Then on May 21, Decca issued a 10" LP (5560) featuring the A and B sides of the first four singles for the company. An EP was also issued about the same time featuring 'Shake, Rattle And Roll', 'Rock Around The Clock', 'Dim, Dim The Lights' and 'Happy Baby'.

But for all the success, Haley's life was not one of unmitigated joy. About now, or earlier, he was crushed by the death of his mother. Public fame and acclaim and private tragedy were to be a recurring theme.

As 'Rock Around The Clock' entered the Top Ten, the act appeared on their most important TV broadcast to date, 'The Milton Berle Show', screened May 31. Other major coast-to-coast TV appearances followed, 'The Sammy Kay Show' and, the pinnacle for all acts, Ed Sullivan's 'Toast Of The Town' (August 7); plus a coast-to-coast NBC radio broadcast with the McGuire Sisters. June saw the act in one-week residencies at the Colonial Tavern in Toronto and Chicago's Regal Theatre, an important black venue, for 'Rock Around The Clock' was now making strong headway in R&B markets. June 25, the record moves 4 to 3 pop, with the report that it has already passed the million sales mark. Yet Decca already release 'Razzle Dazzle' (29552). July 6: Haley is thirty years old and he could not have wished for a better birthday present than the news that 'Rock Around The Clock' had just become the best selling record in the USA, whilst Decca announced to the trade that sales of all his product were already in excess of three million. Meantime other Hollywood film producers were keen to exploit Haley and in July 'Shake, Rattle And Roll' was heard in Sheree North's latest, 'How To Be Very, Very Popular', whilst 'Razzle Dazzle' was to be heard in Mamie Van Doren's next picture, 'Running Wild', out in November. The music, combined with these ladies' charms – whose acting limitations were not stretched in such 'B' film fodder – were doubtless aimed at the same lads currently dancing in the aisles during 'Blackboard Jungle'.

The singer next embarked on his most extensive tour of one-nighters yet, kicking off in Maryland and down to Virginia and the Carolinas before a swing through the Deep South, and then through the mid-West, finishing in Kansas, before a stint in Canada. This was probably the tour on which Hank Snow and Elvis Presley, both currently riding high in the country charts, were added to the southern and mid-western itinerary. It was Col. Tom Parker, friend of Lord Jim Ferguson, who got them on the show, two con-men every inch as phoney as their adopted titles. Presley's repertoire at one time or another included 'Shake, Rattle And Roll' and 'Rock Around The Clock'; yet when J. I. Allison (drummer with the future Crickets) met him in Lubbock and wondered why he had no drums, Presley said, 'Aw, if I had me a drummer I'd sound like Bill Haley.' As Haley's opening act, Presley's three-piece must have seemed sparse, notwithstanding his exciting presence, compared to the star's charged six-piece. Presley wasn't going down well in some places, Haley recalls him as an 'awfully nice kid', but demoralised. Haley believed the problem was his inclusion of ballads; he suggested dropping them and keeping the act strictly rhythmic . Haley himself would never do ballads, 'It's not what the kids want.' The two singers became buddies and would meet again later in the year.

The eventful summer of 1955 also saw 'Razzle Dazzle' reach No. 15 on *Billboard*'s best sellers' list on July 23, whilst 'Clock' was in its third week at No. 1. *Billboard* also reported brisk business for 'Two Hound Dogs'. Another milestone was when *Billboard* (August 6) reported 'Clock' not only No. 1 in the best sellers but also No. 1 in air play and No. 1 in jukebox plays. Previously Haley could never gain anything like parity in all three areas, for pop radio stations feared upsetting listeners with such boisterous music and juke box operators didn't wish to offend the patrons of restaurants and cafes where their equipment was invariably sited. Clearly 'Clock' had overturned all such opposition, thanks no doubt to the popularity of 'Blackboard Jungle'. Meantime the record reached No. 4 in *Billboard*'s R&B best sellers whilst conspicuously failing to make any headway in the country market, a strange irony given Haley's background.

The record's phenomenal success also brought problems. Decca was slapped with a lawsuit from Gotham Records, owners of the original version of 'Rock The Joint' by Jimmy Preston, alleging that 'Rock Around The Clock' was an infringement of its copyright. This was obviously a nonsense, for few people would recognise a similarity between the two records. What 'Clock' is similar to is Haley's own version of 'Rock The Joint', which was so different from Preston's that he could have almost got away with using a different title and claiming composer's royalties for himself. But he didn't, and Gotham did nicely out of the publishing royalty. Rather than being both grateful and realistic, Gotham now reappear years later wanting a piece of the action on something they had no right to. Meanwhile Haley's version had been reissued in July (Essex 399; flip, 'Farewell, So Long, Goodbye') to capitalise on the No. 1 status of 'Clock'. Haley was furious at this latest Essex reissue, the third since his signing with Decca, doubtless because some might be confused by the two records' similarity and ask for the Essex instead. But given the singer's current outstanding success, his concern, let alone anger, seemed hardly justified. Even so, he sought an injunction against Essex. Under the heading, 'Haley Seeking to Restrain Release of Essex Masters', *Cash Box* carried the following report. 'Philadephia, August 6. Bill Haley, current top-selling pop artist, has filed an unusual suit against Dave Miller of Essex Records, Haley's former company. The Decca star is asking the courts to stop Miller from releasing old masters Haley cut while under contract to Essex.

'Haley, in his complaint,' continued the report, 'alleges that his Essex disks are of "inferior quality" to his current releases. Haley's suit also asks that Miller be prevented from using the name "The Comets" on the grounds that the tag belongs to him.

'Miller claims that the Haley group was billed as "The Saddle Men" when he signed them, and that he switched the unit from country & western to rhythm & blues and dubbed them The Comets. He contends that Haley's first Essex records, issued under the Saddle Men tag, were reissued under the Comet monicker while the artist was still under the contract to Miller.

'Haley also asks for an accounting on his Essex releases. However, according to Miller, the only reason he never gave an accounting was that he "wasn't asked", and he is making records available to the artist of this week. Miller, through attorney H. Lipsius, will file a counter-suit as soon as the "Rock Around The Clock" performer concludes an announced plan to amend his original complaint.'

This all sounds like hot air and as we hear no more we can be sure nothing came of it. The only point of interest is the request for an accounting – Haley probably saw little or nothing on record sales' royalties on 'Crazy, Man, Crazy' – in any event a shifty character like Miller would have covered his tracks very carefully on this one.

The earnings from the partnership (Haley, Ferguson, Grande, Williamson) had gone through the roof from the national TV and radio fees, sell-out shows, song royalties, and so on. Haley bought a cadillac for each of the five Comets. For himself he bought a yacht, calling it *Comet,* and went fishing for shark in between appearances at the Steel Pier in Atlantic City and the Starlight and Surf Clubs in Wildwood. The biggest splash of his new found wealth was the commissioning of a purpose-built ranch house with several acres right next to his boyhood home and school. Called 'Melody Manor', it was intended for his mother, according to Milt Gabler, a frequent guest. What amused Gabler was that Haley kept a chicken shack at the front: 'People would come to visit this big star in his big house and he'd have chickens roaming around at the front!' Haley sought to make it a happy home and showered love on his wife and family – for the kids he had a series of maze-like roller skate paths made – with barbecue parties in the summer and great celebrations at Christmas, for not only his family but also the Comets and their families. Home and family were very important to Haley – even more so since Mother died and his father had become seriously ill – and Christmas was the one time he refused to work, no matter how much he was offered.

4. Controversy

But for all his generosity, in August 1955 he lacked imagination and acumen. The partners were living like kings, whilst the wage-earning Comets, Lytle, Richards and Ambrose, were still each on $150 a week plus $42.50 recording session fees, which were not often. Bringing them into the partnership was not a feasible idea – it would have meant a smaller share for everyone – but commonsense dictated that with his new status, their wage should have risen accordingly, particularly because the three guys were an integral part of the stage act and not mere backing musicians. They were shrewd, anticipating Haley's refusal of their request for a pay rise, and resolved to form their own act. Frank Pingatore, writer of two recent Haley songs, became their manager and they secretly attracted the attention of Capitol Records who were more than ready to exploit the Haley connection. September, and Haley still had made no offer, so the boys quit. According to Richards, the departure left no hard feelings – we may think otherwise later – for Haley still needed them to rehearse their replacements.

They became The Jodimars – a clever acronym for Joey, Dick and Marshall – on Capitol with Pingatore writing most of their material. The trio – which became a sextet – did not lack for work and secured lucrative engagements in Las Vegas. A testimony to their success is that they lasted for four years and despite no hits made more money than if they had remained Comets.

The fissure of the Comets occurred whilst 'Rock Around The Clock' was yet No. 1. Earlier, in the August 20 issue of *Billboard*, a clear development could be observed in the trade's national chart. In the wake of Haley, rock'n'roll records by other artists had arrived. Whilst the top records after Haley's were still squaresville (No. 2, Pat Boone's 'Ain't That A Shame' – though to the uninitiated this seemed hep; 3, Mitch Miller's 'Yellow Rose Of Texas'; 4, Frank Sinatra's 'Learning The Blues'; 5, Nat 'King' Cole's 'A Blossom Fell'), rising at numbers 7, 13 and 18 respectively were Boyd Bennett's Haley-like 'Seventeen', Chuck Berry's 'Maybelline' and Fats Domino's original of Pat Boone's hit. The face of pop music was changing!

Meanwhile Haley needed new Comets in a hurry. As luck would have it, the upheaval proved to be an unexpected blessing. For a start, the Comets became a sextet with the introduction of a lead guitarist. Hitherto the stage Comets had no lead guitarist, guitar solos being played on Williamson's steel. Franny Beecher had been Haley's session guitarist, but never a fully fledged Comet because the money wasn't enough. Now Haley offered him $175 a week, whether the group worked or not. Stage uniforms, equipment, and all travelling expenses would be paid, plus the usual studio session fees. Beecher was in. Later, Haley gave him $300 a week, more than some successful solo acts were earning at the time. Beecher later recalled, 'I had three Lincoln Continentals. If one got a little dusty I just traded it in.' Former Haley bassist Al Rex returned to the fold; but finding the right drummer was not so straightforward. Haley wanted Ralph Jones, an excellent jazz drummer whom he knew from his WPWA days; but such was Jones' dislike of rock'n'roll, notwithstanding the fact that he could quit his day job as a milkman and quadruple his income as a Comet, he refused. Haley's drummers in the meantime were Don Raymond and Dean Tinker, but when Jones' close friend Rudy Pompilii, with whom he had worked for many years, joined Haley, Jones changed his mind. Pompilii, a year older than Haley, was from a devout Roman Catholic family in the Italian section of Chester. The clarinet was his favourite instrument, but the saxophone would be his fortune. As a distraught prisoner of war in Europe he vowed to God to try and be 'a better person' if he ever got out. Back home, he quickly made a name for himself and national recognition beckoned when he toured, but apparently didn't record, with the Ralph Marterie Orchestra (the same band which had covered 'Crazy, Man, Crazy'). Readers of *Downbeat* magazine voted him the 'Most Promising New Saxophonist' of 1953, leading to Pompilii's proudest moment at the magazine's awards' ceremony when he played with Duke Ellington. From Duke Ellington to Bill Haley was a long way, and some would say a deep drop; but Pompilii's spirit, though he idolised the likes of Benny Goodman and John Coltrane, was somewhere else. He was an extrovert, a showman: raising his back, he would make his instrument soar and scream as he dropped to his knees and lay on his back. Such an act did not belong to the sophisticated world of swing and jazz. This was R&B territory. Enter Bill Haley.

Rudy Pompilii would become the best known Comet of all: Haley's right hand man and best friend. But ultimately Haley didn't deserve Pompilii and if there is any hero in our story it is this wonderful man.

Haley had Rudy's name spelt 'Pompilli' right from the start, not something the saxophonist was happy about, for he could see that, spelt correctly, it might be seen as a printer's error or it would be mispelt anyway. The enlarged Comets brought changes to the stage act. Franny Beecher would have his own solo spot – a fast boogie – and he had an unexpected talent: he could sing like a five year old girl! This was after the straight-faced Haley would announce to the audience that he was 'one of the finest baritones he had ever heard'. Beecher would also form a comic trio with Williamson and Rex, he delivering a high tenor lead in an Ink Spots spoof. The comedy was invariably devised by Williamson who was the act's main ideas' man. Haley would play the straight man to the antics and tomfoolery of the others. Rex worked particularly hard. He would play double bass lying down; he would swing it in the air, climb it, play it on his back and, when straddling it, Pompilii with screaming sax would perch on his back. Such antics were hazardous and several times Rex narrowly missed serious injury: once he fell when climbing his double bass and the instrument tumbled across the stage, its neck breaking. Rex picked up the neck and pretended to play it: the kids went wild, thinking it was all part of the act. He also ran the risk of splitting his pants, but that too would be seen as part of the act. Rex, drenched in sweat, hair tossed over his face, then immediately had to take centre stage as lead vocalist whilst Haley slapped bass. What a sight! Instead of a breather, Rex had to perform a mandatory three torrid numbers – invariably Little Richard! – and sometimes up to six.

They were the loudest band in the country, audiences would wonder what hit them. At Decca's Pythian studio, where performers would record on stage, invited guests would soon leave when hearing the almighty racket of Haley's combo! But Gabler loved them. Haley was the star, but the Comets were the show. Unlike in Britain in 1957, the show would last between 45 and 80 minutes, and for only half or less of that time Haley sang. He would sing only the hits, for he could hardly delegate these to the others.

The new ensemble performed their first show on Wednesday, September 21. For the next two days they were in the studio to record two new singles. On the Thursday they cut 'R.O.C.K.', which Haley had co-written with Rusty and Ruth Keefer (Rusty was once Haley's guitarist in the early Aces of Western Swing days), and 'Rock-A-Beatin' Boogie', a Haley number first recorded by Danny Cedrone in 1952. Friday, they cut 'Saints' Rock'n'Roll' – though a traditional song, was given composer credits of 'Haley-Gabler' on account of the new lyric – and 'Burn That Candle', a cover version of The Cubs' new record, a black vocal group on Capitol. I say 'new ensemble', but that's not exactly true, for again Haley offended his drummer by substituting jazz session man Cliff Leeman. Of these four new sides, three contain the word 'rock', Haley exploiting the new idiom for all its worth and his role in it, celebrated in the clever lyric of 'R.O.C.K.'. Rudy Pompilii announces his arrival to the world with his searing intro to 'Rock-A-Beatin' Boogie', before an exciting exchange with Beecher. The two are name-checked on 'Saints' with their own solo spots, and whilst Rex isn't mentioned he blasts to the fore, showing all that no-one in the world can slap bass like he.

October was another eventful month. Elvis Presley reappears and Buddy Holly appears in our narrative. The sequence and details are unclear, for the sources are inconsistent. On the 19th and 20th, Haley was in Cleveland to appear in a short documentary film (amazingly never released, neither then nor since) which also featured Presley and others. Local DJ Tommy Edwards took a photo of Presley with Haley, a picture which Haley would display in his 'Melody Manor' office for many years. Haley stands left in a red tuxedo and black bow-tie, looking every inch the star and gushing with confidence, whilst Presley, in brown jacket and open neck shirt looks like the hot new kid on the block. I love this picture: both men are obviously at ease with one another and both are at the peak of their artistic powers. When the rock'n'roll magazine *Now Dig This* published its 100th edition, it put this picture on its front cover. No wonder. The same month, Buddy Holly, as one half of a duo, was the opening act when Haley played at the Fair Park Coloseum in Dallas. But Haley, in an interview years later, recalled performing in Lubbock with Buddy Holly *backing him*! As Haley recalls it, he had arrived with Ferguson in their own car for a concert at the local stadium. The Comets were behind in another vehicle and were delayed because of a flat tyre. The show was late and the audience was restless. Holly, who was presumably an opening act, offered to help Haley out of his dilemma by going on stage with him with some others – whom Haley presumed to be the Crickets, but if this was 1955, this could not have been the case. So, for half an hour, until the Comets arrived, Buddy Holly was Bill Haley's sideman! It reveals Holly's familiarity with the Haley repertoire, but more likely Haley opened with 'Shake, Rattle And Roll' and then got Holly to sing tunes he knew, whilst he played rhythm, which is what he did with the Comets anyway. Haley took a big liking to the lad: he said it 'was a long time later' before they met again – at Decca's offices in New York where they had a 'big reunion', and later they met again on tour in Jacksonville, Florida.

'Rock Around The Clock' meanwhile had passed the three million sales mark. During the summer it had spent eight consecutive weeks at No. 1 on *Billboard*'s best sellers chart and was No.1 on even the airplay chart for six seeks, a remarkable feat given pop stations' hostility to rock'n'roll. By October 22 the record had completed 24 consecutive weeks in *Billboard*'s Top 25 best sellers, whilst in Britain – the first place anywhere to make it a hit, back in January – it made a new appearance in the Top Twenty following the recent release of 'Blackboard Jungle' in cinemas. It entered *NME*'s chart October 15, a chart on which the Top Three was occupied by Jimmy Young, Frank Sinatra and Mitch Miller, for not-withstanding Haley, Britain remained deep in squaresville. On the 29th, it moved 8 to 7, the same date American trade journals reported strong reaction to the act's latest single, the sixth on Decca (29713). *Billboard*: 'For speedy take-off, Haley is still the man to beat. Most territories have had this record only a week, but the immediate response in the stores and in juke boxes has been solid.' The trade then tells of solid action throughout the north-east and also breakouts in the south (Durham) and west to Chicago, Nashville and St Louis. 'Customers eager for the record', continued *Billboard*, 'so far have not indicated a clear preference for the top side, though "Rock-A-Beatin' Boogie" does have an early edge.' Yet it was the flip, 'Burn That Candle' which shot into the trade's Top 100 at No. 46 on November 12, the highest new entry in the first week of the inaugural chart. Prior to this date, there existed only the various separate sales, jukebox and airplay charts consisting of just 20 to 30 positions. *Billboard* continued to publish these along with the new Top 100 – later famously re-titled as the 'Hot 100' – which was a fusion of sales, airplay and juke box spins. 'Rock-A-Beatin' Boogie' was in at No. 62, whilst 'Clock' was at 31. Two weeks later, on the 26th, 'Rock-A-Beatin' Boogie' had reached its peak position of No. 41, whilst 'Candle' was at 38 and 'Clock' at 57. In Britain, on the same date, 'Clock' reached No. 1, displacing the Johnston Brothers' 'Hernando's Hideaway'. Meanwhile, Haley and the Comets were packing them in wherever they went. November 23-27, at Brooklyn's Paramount, they topped a bill that included Johnnie Ray and LaVern Baker, the shows grossing a total of $55,000. December 3, 4000 showed up for two shows at the Keith Theatre in Baltimore, whilst on the 17th and 18th they played the Court Square Theatre in Springfield, Massachusetts, breaking the house record with a two-day take of $5000. The previous week, on the 12th, they were unexpectedly in the studio for another single. Although their next single, 'Saints Rock'n'Roll'/ 'R-O-C-K' was already in the can, there had been a development. Two weeks earlier, Chess Records had issued 'Later, Alligator' by Bobby Charles which was already breaking out in the mid-West. Charles, whose real name was Guidry, had also written the song, which the gutsy 14-year old had previously pitched to Fats Domino whose reaction was, 'Alligator? I don't know nothin' about alligators, man.' But Guidry was lucky for Domino who later recorded his 'I'm Walking To New Orleans'; likewise, Clarence 'Frogman' Henry found international fame with Guidry's 'But I Do'. Milt Gabler was convinced that the 'Alligator' catch phrase could be a smash for Haley and he wanted him on it immediately. There was no time to book the Pythian, so a rush session was arranged at Decca's other studio on the second floor of their office building. This was the only Haley record not done at the Pythian, but you wouldn't know it, for the sound was exactly the same. The mood must have been euphoric: the dull – by comparison – Charles version transmuted into a chorus blast of the catch phrase and the full might of Pompilii, Beecher and Williamson on the instrumental break. Here was the Haley magic triumphant: just as he had thrillingly metamorphosed 'Rock The Joint', 'Rock Around The Clock' and 'Shake, Rattle And Roll', he made 'See You Later, Alligator' completely his own. Yes, he was a 'covers' act', yet paradoxically an originator. The dozens of white cover acts of the day merely diluted R&B: Haley always metamorphosed 'R&B/R&R' into pure R&R, a true musical alchemist. And nor was the Haley-Gabler magic ever better: Gabler, who understood the singer perfectly, knew 'Alligator' was a song tailor made for him and could imagine a fully charged Comets arrangement. Bobby Charles was not robbed of a hit – it is unlikely he would have ever seen a cent from sales of his record anyway – but Haley provided him with an income for the rest of his life. Probably no-one at the session was happier than Ralph Jones, who for once was allowed to drum on record. He had been understandably peeved that Haley preferred Decca's session drummers to him, but this time the singer relented after the intervention of Billy Gussack. Decca percussionist Gussack had seen Jones on stage and told Haley that he could see absolutely no reason why he couldn't record. This was a curious situation, for it was Haley who was so keen to recruit Jones as a Comet in the first place; but it seems that the root of his anxiety was that as rhythm guitarist he depended on the drummer to lead, and as all his hits had been with session drummers he didn't want to break a winning formula. Haley was encouraged by Gabler in this view and when Jones showed up for the session, before any of the other Comets had played a note, the producer first tested his rimshot. Haley and Gabler would have no regrets. The more than credible 'B' side, 'The Paper Boy (On Main Street, USA)' was written by Cathryn Cafra, wife of Billy Williamson, which was more likely his composition, the song being placed in her name as a tax dodge.

Saturday, December 31, the act played in Detroit, earning $2500. The same date on Britain's *NME* chart showed 'Rock Around The Clock' at No. 2, temporarily dislodged from the top by Dickie Valentine's 'Christmas Alphabet', whilst 'Rock-A-Beatin' Boogie' was at No. 21. In the issue dated December 31, *Billboard* ran Decca's whole page for 'See You Later, Alligator' (Decca 29791), the label wisely adding 'See You' to the published title. The label also issued a version (29786) of the song by Roy Hall, cut in Nashville and aimed at the country market. With Haley, Decca were going for the pop and R&B markets, the irony being that Haley, the ex-country crooner, could not, unlike Elvis Presley, sell into the country market. The same issue showed 'Burn That Candle' at its peak position of No. 20 on the Top 100 and as high as No. 12 on the jukebox chart. Also in the same issue, was a report concerning a forthcoming film, 'Rock Around The Clock' featuring Haley, Alan Freed, The Platters and others, that 'Jimmy Myers' had 'completed a deal with Columbia Pictures for the use of his title'. What a scream! Not only does the publisher make a bundle on the inclusion of 'Clock' and other Myers copyrights in the film, he graciously 'allows' Columbia to use his title (more big bucks!). Talk about 'money for old rope'. Thanks to Haley, Myers was getting richer not just by the day, but by the minute! The film was effectively a 'B' feature, shot on a low budget and within two weeks – Haley's involvement lasted only a few days – the bulk of the cost probably being on Myers' fee, Haley ($120,000) and Freed's name, which interestingly enough in Alan's case, rhymes with 'greed'. Haley and the boys arrived in Hollywood on January 3, after a 37-hour ride from Chicago on the *Sante Fe Super Chef*. January 7 saw a strengthening of Haley's position in the UK as 'Clock' returned to No. 1 and 'Rock-A-Beatin' Boogie' soared from 21 to 5. Decca LP 8345 originally released as 'Shake, Rattle And Roll', but then re-titled 'Rock Around The Clock', was approaching its top placing of No. 12 on *Billboard*'s albums' chart, whilst 'Clock', the single, now passed the four-million sales' mark, thanks to its UK success.

The January 14 issue of *Billboard* showed 'See You Later, Alligator' leaping into the Top 100 at 56 and already No. 25 in sales. 'Burn That Candle' was at No. 20, in its tenth week in the 100, whilst the flip was at 61. In Britain, the *NME* of the same date placed 'Clock' in its fifth and final week at No. 1 – about to be replaced by Tennessee Ernie Ford's '16 Tons' – whilst 'Rock-A-Beatin' Boogie' was at No. 4, its best position, being stopped from going higher by Bill Hayes' 'Ballad Of Davy Crockett' and Frank Sinatra's 'Love And Marriage'. Suddenly Haley was bigger in Britain than in the States and negotiations were afoot for a UK tour to begin at the London Palladium in June. For reasons unknown, the tour didn't materialise: most likely, either Haley's fee was too high or the UK Musicians' Union objected, that objectionable organisation which deprived British rock'n'roll fans of seeing so many Americans. After Hollywood, Haley rested a few days in Las Vegas, he and wife Cuppy managing to enjoy themselves despite losses in the casinos. On route home, at Salt Lake City, Haley found 'See You Later, Alligator' already in the local Top Ten and performed two sell-out shows (January 21). Next, on the Union Pacific's *City of Los Angeles*, the entourage enjoyed the 15-hour ride through Utah, Wyoming and the Rocky Mountains, before arriving in Chicago, where 'they couldn't find a hotel' (Haley's diary) and all nine were cramped for one night in a single room: an odd circumstance for the man whom show-biz weekly *Variety* would describe as the 'highest paid entertainer in the world'.

Cash Box had speculated that Haley's income in 1955 from personal appearances was $500,000 (which obviously would equate to many millions in today's money); and then there were his TV and radio fees and his considerable income from song royalties. In a nine-day tour of the South beginning in late January, his earnings were over $14,000. But, as we know, Haley's earnings from shows weren't all for himself: they were split four ways between himself, Ferguson, Grande and Williamson. They had become wealthy men and together their business interests extended beyond the music, for they also owned an art gallery and a small steel mill, Industrial Mechanics, which employed six or seven men. Haley and Ferguson in particular viewed business as a means of making money for little effort – which in the music world was often very true – but in point of fact as businessmen they would prove incompetent. The steel mill wouldn't last long and Ferguson managed to alienate a merchandiser who could have made them much richer still through the marketing of Haley T-shirts, wallets, ties, and so on. As we shall see, between them Haley and Ferguson couldn't organise the proverbial booze-up in a brewery. Their centre of operations was a house on Chester's Fifth Street where they had a recording studio and at the top on the third floor Haley had his office with desk elevated, 'so you had to look up at him like Hitler' (Jim Feddis). Feddis was hired to run a talent booking agency they had started: this, too, would end up in trouble. At this juncture, we know that Haley owned, or co-owned at least two music publishing ventures, one, Valleybrook Music, receiving payments through the long established royalties' collection agency ASCAP, and the other, Seebreeze Music, through BMI.

After a highly successful short tour of the South – including record sell-outs in Birmingham and Charlotte – Haley was back home on February 6, where he rested for a week before driving with wife and family to Miami Beach and the sun; a trip presumably made in his new 1956 Fleetwood Cadillac; 'the most gorgeous car I've ever seen', he entered in his diary. Such was his love of home and family that he turned down $5000 for an appearance on 'The Milton Berle TV Show' which would have interrupted his three-week vacation. During this time 'Alligator' had entered *Billboard*'s national R&B chart, reaching No. 14; and reaching No. 6 Pop. In *Cash Box*'s pop chart of March 7 it went to No. 5. February 29, the boys were in Toronto for the 'Cross Canada Hit Parade' TV show, netting Haley $2000, before they were off for a two-week tour of the mid-West. Haley's attention to detail is apparent in his diary entries: at St Louis (March 2) there were '14 less' in attendance compared to his last appearance there, and at Chicago's Oregon Ballroom (March 13), '1500 people here. Not good, but great for this place on a Tuesday night'. A week earlier, at Omaha in Nebraska, he broke all records for one show, picking up $3500 for his efforts; but in Wisconsin he lost on cancelled shows when his troupe became snowbound. On the same week – with 'Alligator' still firmly placed in the Top Ten, his latest single, 'R-O-C-K'/'Saints Rock'n'Roll' (Decca 29870), was released. Haley was in Washington, DC, for the world premier of 'Rock Around The Clock' (March 14). It opened in a blaze of publicity at three cinemas. Despite the show-biz razzamatazz, Haley and wife were still on the 11.00 train home. A charming insight gleaned from his diaries is his yen for domesticity. Even when he was recording in New York, he would always be on the 6.30 train home to Chester, eager to see wife and kids. Imagine, you could be on your way home on the 6.30 and the fellow who sits next to you just happens to be ... Bill Haley. He was in the lobby of the Stanley Theatre at 9.30 (15th) for the Philadelphia premier, but atrocious weather kept patrons away and he left half an hour later. But despite a blizzard, he played to 6000 the next night in Hartford, Connecticut, then 8000 the following night, after which he and Cuppy caught the midnight train home. The next few days he was snowed in at 'Melody Manor'. In between digging out driveways and walks he worked on songs for another milestone: his first (proper) album.

The week from March 27 was to be an eventful one. On that date, in the Pythian studio, starting at 10.00, half of the album was recorded. Then, Haley's weekend was split between rehearsing for the rest of the album and visiting sister Peggy who was taking care of their infirm father. On Sunday he wrote in his diary, 'Early to bed as tomorrow's a big day.' And the big day was ... an important TV show? Interview? No – it was his daughter Joanie's third birthday. 'Thank you, Lord, for this wonderful little girl', he wrote in his diary. 'She is worth more than all the success in the world.' All the Comets, their wives and kids, were there for Joanie's day.

It is very hard not to like this man.

On the Tuesday (28th) morning at Decca, they laid down three of the LP's best tracks, 'Choo Choo Ch' Boogie', 'Calling All Comets' and 'Blue Comet Blues', before six hours of rehearsals for 'The Arthur Godfrey TV Show', which was to be shot the following night. The next morning, driving to New York for more TV rehearsals, Haley completed 'Hot Dog Buddy Buddy', a song which he was rightly pleased with and which Gabler saw as the next hit single he needed from the album sessions. That night on the TV show, the act performed 'Rudy's Rock' and 'Alligator', Godfrey presenting Haley with a gold record for one million sales of the latter.

'See You Later, Alligator' meanwhile was already heading for its second million when on March 10 in Britain it leapt into the *NME* Top 20 at No. 9. Despite such a promising start, it would go no higher than No. 7, it residing seven weeks in the Top Ten.

After the Godfrey show — for which Haley received $2500 — he spent the following day (29th) relaxing and shopping for Easter gifts for the kids. Good Friday (30th), he was very pleased to have finished the album with the recording of 'Rockin' Through The Rye', 'Hot Dog Buddy Buddy' and 'A Rockin' Little Tune'. He was home early at 6.00, enjoying dinner with Cuppy and Bob Hayes, his song publishing representative in the mid-West, the three rounding off the evening with a trip to the local cinema. The Easter weekend was spent between work and family. Of the Saturday he wrote, 'Got the kids baskets and candy, then bought a new 1956 Plymouth Savoy sport coupe. Red and white. New cars are my biggest expense. Ho, ho.' That night he performed to 3112 people at Asbury Park, New Jersey, making $1750. Easter Sunday, he was in his element surrounded by his family and proud of his little son wearing his first suit when they visited Jim Ferguson's ailing mother. Then there was a great feast in the Haley household before a family outing to the pictures. April began with a week's residency at the Twin Coaches in Pittsburgh, interspersed with TV and radio appearances. He writes in his diary of giving up to five encores, and we might marvel at the luck of the Twin Coaches audiences. Also in his diary at this point, is his record of the progress of 'R-O-C-K' and 'Saints Rock & Roll' on *Billboard*'s charts. These brought his tally of hits for Decca to 14 in just under two years, for virtually every one of his eight singles was a double-sided success. April 7, the single was already at No. 21 on the national sales chart, with both sides listed in this position, whilst on the Top 100 'Saints Rock & Roll' entered at 67 and 'R-O-C-K' at 79. The lower placings on the 100 reflected again the reluctance of many radio stations to play Haley, for air play was a vital component of the chart.

The music industry and certain elements of the general public had by Spring 1956 worked themselves up into a fever of anxiety over rock'n'roll. More kids than ever had latched on to the new music and not a week passed without alarming reports and comment on its alleged corrosive effect. Rock'n'roll was turning youngsters into savages with its primal beat and gibberish lyrics, so it was thought: but more to the point were the deeper implications for racist America. The music was breaking down barriers. Haley was viewed with contempt because he was playing what was considered black music, and worse still, he was selling *to a black audience.* Even *Downbeat* readers had voted him 'R&B Personality of the Year', placing him ahead of the likes of Ray Charles, Bo Diddley, Chuck Berry, Joe Turner, and so on. Haley had been the main culprit, but more southern white boys had come to national prominence with their own brand of 'nigger bop', Carl Perkins and Elvis Presley who had also been embraced by young blacks. But there was much worse: a demon had broken out of hell: its name was Little Richard and white boys and girls were mesmerised. Previously, Pat Boone could be counted on to shield American youth from Fats Domino and Little Richard, but now, with 'Long Tall Sally', all defences had been breached. From the viewpoint of the established order, Haley was seen as merely 'vulgar', Presley 'disgusting', but Little Richard was simply 'naked savagery' – the last straw. Moreover, the phenomenon was not helped by its association with violence: started by 'Blackboard Jungle' and compounded by 'Rock Around the Clock', kids everywhere dancing in cinema aisles, swept away in a modern version of the St Vitus Dance. Police were summoned by anxious cinema managers and order was not always restored peacefully. Moreover the thuggish elements in youth culture gleefully attached themselves to the new music, compounding its sinister reputation amongst the 'respectable'. Haley therefore found himself in a predicament when he headlined the 'Biggest Rock'n'Roll Show of 1956', a 47-day nationwide tour on which all the other acts were black: Shirley & Lee, The Drifters, The Five Keys, Bo Diddley, LaVern Baker, The Turbans, The Platters, Roy Hamilton, and most interestingly in terms of our subject, Big Joe Turner. A late signing was Frankie Lymon & The Teenagers who were brought in to close the show's first half on account of their current smash, 'Why do Fools Fall In Love?'. Such a line-up, Haley recognised, was going to attract legions of both white and black kids and he was deeply troubled by the implications when the tour hit the Deep South. Tour promoter Irving Feld told *Billboard* that the show's first five days (beginning April 20) had grossed $100,000 in receipts and he was fully confident of a total gross of a million on the six weeks. More important, was Feld's report that there had been no incidents and audiences were well behaved. Not strictly true, for at Scranton, Pennsylvania, Haley was mobbed as he was leaving the stage, sustaining an injury near his eye, particularly alarming for a man with limited vision. Two nights later in White Plains, New York, he got mobbed and hit again. For the first week, he was able to return home every night, as all shows were in the North-East, but when this was no longer possible he was immediately gripped by misgivings: show-biz and touring could never mean as much to him as the warmth of wife, home and family. It was at this time he received another offer to go to Britain, this time from the Grades in London: $20,000 for two weeks, but he refused. When 'The Biggest Rock'n'Roll Show of 1956' played to sold-out houses in Montreal and Toronto, Haley was besieged by Canadian radio, TV and newspaper reporters. 'Is rock'n'roll harming teenagers?' He was getting sick of this type of question, yet he was always patient and diplomatic in his response. His line of argument was always the same and perfectly sound: because kids love the beat and the exciting rhythms doesn't make them 'savages', on the contrary it's a healthy outlet; each new generation upsets the old when it adopts something 'outrageous', 30 years earlier people were outraged by the Charleston, swing music, and so on; today it is rock'n'roll and in another 30 years it will be something else. The kids want excitement and fun, yet they are well behaved; only a tiny minority are violent and they discredit both the majority and the music. To Haley, his music was fun and actually a force for good: he was extremely annoyed and frustrated that no matter what he, Alan Freed, or anyone else said, the media continued to emphasise the negative aspect.

Despite the isolated violent incidents, Haley was by and large pleased with the kids' behaviour on this tour; but back in New York State – in Rochester of all places – a 'plot' was foiled to pull the singer off stage: but this was not by rock'n'roll fans, but by white racist thugs. May 2 in Buffalo saw the novelty of Haley's film opening in a local cinema to a capacity audience of 3000 at the very same moment 9000 were packed into see him in the flesh a few blocks away! No wonder this tour was a pot of gold for the promoter: Haley now had the added aura of being a film star, a film star who was not remote and walled up in Hollywood, but who could actually be seen in the flesh in one's own home town! The tour next swung through

Ohio and Michigan with few incidents. In Detroit, Haley's childhood home town, he was reunited with Kenny Roberts who taught him so many yodelling tricks and whom he had replaced in The Downliners back in '44. Roberts himself was now also recording for Decca, at their country studios in Nashville. It was at this time Haley received another film offer: RKO wanted him for an Eddie Fisher-Debbie Reynolds musical, but he had to decline because of prior engagements. After an all-night 540-mile drive from Omaha to Denver, where it was a sold-out 9000, at midnight began another long haul: the 840 miles to Dallas. Twenty-six days into the tour, the boys were getting worn down by the travelling; Al Rex took sick and could not carry on. Haley's own entourage consisted of 12 persons, including himself and the band; but it seems that all but one of this additional personnel had dropped out by the time they got to Dallas. That Haley seemed to manage without them suggests they were not necessary in the first place, and we will return to this point. During this tour, Haley had – purposely – lost a stone in weight; The Comets also dieted and we may remark at this joint effort of self-discipline at a time when the temptation to drink and eat was that much greater with morale flagging and the disorientation of endless travel and sleeping in vehicles. Indeed by Dallas, Haley himself wondered how much more of this he could take, while an oblivious Jolly Joyce continuously pressured him to take on more, for booking agent Joyce the Haley phenomenon was also a pot of gold. But by the time he got to New Orleans (May 19), after a 400-mile drive from Houston, his spirits were lifted when Cuppy joined him for 12 days of the tour. In New Orleans, he met Fats Domino, these two rock'n'rollers taking an immediate liking to one another. Perhaps Cuppy came at this time to help his morale through the part of the tour he dreaded most: the Deep South. The long overnight drive from New Orleans to Birmingham, Alabama, saw an ill omen: their truck overturned, injuring three Comets, but they were still able to go on with the show. The Ku Klux Klan were out in force, picketing the Birmingham venue, their intimidation ensuring that the house was half full. There was also a low turnout at the next venue in Chattanooga, Tennessee; and the following night in Greenville, South Carolina, one of the two scheduled shows was cancelled when a bomb was discovered in the auditorium. However, the following dates in Atlanta (10,000 at an open air venue), Jacksonville, Tampa, Miami (14,000, outdoors), all went well without incident; then a surprise at Savannah, Georgia, when this time it was negroes boycotting the show, leading to a cancellation: an act which directly harmed the black performers whose income depended on these shows and not on record royalties. Heading east on the 29th, the show broke all attendance records with 14,000 at Charlotte and 6,000 were turned away. The final week, playing in Virginia, Washington, DC and Pennsylvania was also highly successful and without incident, and a shattered Bill Haley finally arrived home on Wednesday, June 5.

While Haley was on tour, tired, anxious, pining for home and family, fretting about his ailing father, his fame and wealth were increasing by the day. The May 12 issue of *Billboard* showed both sides of the current single at its highest position of No. 16 on the jukebox chart, the same issue also carrying a whole page ad by Decca thanking jukebox operators for their support. A nice touch in this ad is the mention of Jack Howard as Decca's promotion man in Pennsylvania: how far Haley and Howard had come since the days of selling records at barn dances! The single had reached 18 on the sales chart: again both sides were listed together, rather than separately, *Billboard* at the time being still unsure how to treat double-sided hits. In sales, 'Saints' had the edge, but in the Top 100 'R-O-C-K' was always the stronger side, it having reached 29 whilst 'Saints', shown separately had reached 48. In Britain, on May 26, 'Saints' had entered the *NME* chart at No. 23 (the pop weekly had extended its list to 30 places), whilst 'Alligator' was at 22. A further development was the spectacular success of 'Rock Around The Clock' in Germany: it was 22 weeks in the Top 10, made No. 1, and became the first American single to sell a million copies in that country. All sales of 'Clock' had now topped the five million mark: no wonder in every picture of James Myers we see him beaming from ear to ear!

In the June 16 issue of *Billboard*, with 'R-O-C-K' yet at No. 72 in the Top 100, the ninth Decca single, 'Hot Dog, Buddy, Buddy' (29948; flip: 'Rockin' Through The Rye') entered at 82, whilst four places above saw the debut of Gene Vincent and 'Be Bop A Lula'. The following week, Vincent's record zoomed to 43 whilst Haley's was disappointedly at 95. But it recovered and later made it to 60. It really deserved to do better, though in point of fact sales were split as the flip charted too, making 78. It has been said that 'Hot Dog, Buddy, Buddy' is the same as 'Blue Suede Shoes': hum the opening verses of both and the similarity is apparent, and later in the lyric Haley actually mentions Perkins' title. But it is still very much his song and arrangement, the idea for it coming from another teenage catch phrase he had heard.

But none of this really mattered to Bill Haley at the time. He was touring in Canada when on Father's Day, June 17, he received the news that his father had died. He was crushed, for now he had lost both parents, both from cruel and painful illness. Neither was of any great age and we hear, too, that he loses a sister. All these premature losses of family crucified him, and there was something else: a still-born child.

Somewhere in his mind lay an unavoidable connection between great success and great grief. This cruel dichotomy would eventually tear him apart. And underlying all this was the awful realisation that God chose not to answer his prayers, but to punish him instead. Was the punishment a corollary of success? He must have felt this keenly when on the very eve of his father's death, he was feted as royalty in Winnipeg, Manitoba, with a great parade in his and The Comets' honour. At the moment of his exultation, he is told of Dad's death.

Anyone grown in religious indoctrination – Haley's mother was a key member of the local church – is unlikely to feel entirely comfortable with a state of fame and wealth The simple religious belief of unpretentious hard-working folk, more familiar with hardship than extravagance, cannot be easily reconciled with worldly success. The imagery of the celibate, suffering Christ and the burden of 'original sin' do not sit well with the fame, sex and money ethos.

Understandably, such tragedy bound him still closer to his children and the pain of separation from them as a result of his success was even deeper.

He resumed his Canadian tour on June 23 and in Vancouver pulled his biggest fee for a single date yet: $4250, remarkable for an audience of 1000. Dates in Oregon and Washington followed, then a two-day stint at Salt Lake City before heading home.

July 12, the boys were in the Pythian for their next single, 'Rip It Up' and 'Teenager's Mother (Are You Right?)' (Decca 29791). 'Rip It Up' was the first time Haley covered a *bona fide* R&R hit. The Little Richard original already had a head start, having jumped into the Top 100 the previous week at 56. A month later, Haley's version entered at 70, and for the first three weeks of September both versions were simultaneously in the Top 40. Meanwhile 'Teenager's Mother' also charted, making it to No. 67. In *Cash Box*, Richard made it to No. 21 (August 11) and Haley to 24 (September 18). Two classic versions of a classic rock'n'roll song. It didn't matter which one you picked, but hep cats would have bought both. I mentioned earlier a wonderful photo of Haley with Presley; another one is Haley with Richard, taken when the two were filming 'Don't Knock The Rock'. The film's shaky plot reflected the current controversy over R&R and its alleged corrupting effect on teenagers. 'Rip It Up' was one of Haley's numbers in the picture, but Richard steals the film with 'Tutti Frutti' and 'Long Tall Sally'. Haley had his few lines of awkward dialogue, his lack of screen charisma being all too obvious. Despite two successful films, celluloid was not his natural medium; yet it was a different matter on TV of which some surviving footage demonstrates charisma and excitement.

Meanwhile in the UK, summer 1956, Haley's first film, 'Rock Around The Clock', went on general release, whilst 'Saints Rock'n'Roll climbed to No. 5 in *NME*'s Top 30; and when 'Rockin' Through The Rye' leapt into the chart at No. 8 on August 18, again Haley had two records simultaneously in the British Top Ten. The film was shown in 300 cinemas without incident, but suddenly in September, London became the focal point of disturbances. Teddy Boys were dancing in the aisles, whilst others ran to the stage gyrating in front of the image of their hero on the screen. Removed by the management, who invariably had to call in the police, there was further trouble when Teds couldn't get their money back. Whenever this film was showing, the risk of Teddy Boy gangs loitering around cinema doors was present, leading to its ban in several places. Another menace was yobs taking knives to cinema seats, taking the call to 'rip it up' all too literally, an offence which would have horrified the man of whom they were sup- posed to be fans. Youths who pore over every detail of their treasured Brunswick and London-American 78s are unlikely to be the same ones who vandalise others' property. Inevitably the popular press had a field day with this controversy, whilst a more balanced perspective came from an unexpected source, the newspaper of the

Establishment, *The Times*, which pointed out that unruly youths were hardly a new phenomenon and that to blame Haley would be like blaming Mozart and Beethoven for the senseless actions of a minority at the Last Night of The Proms. It was this controversy that suddenly made Bill Haley a household name in Britain. Hitherto he was just another American with a few hit records in Britain, known mainly to teenagers and some of their parents. But the pop music landscape was, almost overnight it seems, experiencing a dramatic change: September 1956 and fully a quarter of the British Hit Parade was occupied by rock'n'roll. Haley's musical invasion had now been reinforced not only by Presley, but also by Gene Vincent, Fats Domino and others. Previously the chart would contain two, three, or at most four, rock records – and these usually by Haley and/or Presley – but now some 25 per cent of the pop market was being taken over by a music form totally unknown less than two years earlier. The *New Musical Express* (*NME*) rushed out a 4-page supplement with their September 21 issue in support of R&R, unlike the other music weeklies such as the *Melody Maker* which loathed it and considered it a passing fad. Clearly the *NME* editor had imagination and vision, seeing that a new generation of record buyers with new tastes signified a major potential for *NME* readership; the pop weekly would dominate its field for years to come.

The *NME* supplement may have been prompted by another dramatic development: a sudden surge in demand for Bill Haley's records. In the same issue, 'See You Later, Alligator', which had vacated the chart in June, was back in at No. 21, whilst 'Rock Around The Clock' reappeared at 17. A third record from the film, 'Razzle Dazzle', was also climbing the chart. Then from September 28 (the chart was always dated a day after the issue date), *for four consecutive weeks, Haley had five separate singles in the Top Twenty*. Whilst 25 per cent of the market was now R&R, Haley alone took a quarter of the Top 20 action! 'Rockin' Through The Rye' had already reached No. 3 and 'Saints' was still solid after a remarkable five months on the chart, whilst 'Razzle Dazzle' would reach 13 and the resuscitated 'Alligator' and 'Clock' reached 13 and 5 respectively. Also benefiting from the film's success were The Platters and Freddie Bell and The Bell Boys. Interestingly, Bell's record, 'Giddy Up A-Ding Dong', would go Top Five in Britain, but not even make the Top 100 in the States. Like Haley, Bell's greatest success was in Britain, a success which also could not be sustained.

Presley was not far behind Haley's British lead. Since he debuted in the UK Hit Parade in May, Presley had not been out of the chart for one single week, registering eight entries. However as the year progressed, Haley gained the ascendancy with sales 15 to 20 per cent ahead of Presley. But it was not like that at all in the States. There, Haley had just one Top Ten hit for the whole year, compared to five Top Three's by Presley; moreover, both Presley albums went to No. 1, whereas Haley's didn't even crack the LP Top 40.

The latter half of 1956 saw Haley's schedule as intense as ever. The summer included a record-breaking residency at Atlantic City's Steel Pier; headlining a show at the record industry's 'Diamond Jubilee' ten-day exposition at New York

City's Coloseum; various state fair engagements. Then followed another lengthy nationwide and Canadian tour beginning September 28 at Hersey in Pennsylvania, Haley once more topping an 'all-coloured' bill which again featured Frankie Lymon & The Teenagers and The Platters; also The Drifters, Clyde McPhatter, The Flairs and Shirley Gunter and The Queens, all of whom were backed by the Buddy Johnson Band. A few days in Canada and the tour had a ten day hiatus until October 11, during which time the boys cut 'Don't Knock The Rock' (the film version was recorded in Hollywood), written by Frank Carger and Roland E. Kent, who do not reappear on any other Haley credits. The same session produced a revival of Danny Overbea's '40 Cups of Coffee' which emphasised Haley's mastery of the R&B idiom, though he is eclipsed by Franny Beecher's thrilling performance. The following week, Decca, exploiting the release of 'Rock'n'Roll Stage Show' LP, put out 'Rudy's Rock', backed with 'Blue Comet Blues' (30085), which quickly appeared on the Top 100 (October 24 chart, November 3 issue of *Billboard*), whilst 'Rip It Up' was yet at 84. The next week it disappointingly fell twenty places to 99 alongside 'Rip It Up' at 98. Then it rallied sharply, reaching 34 on November 24, when Decca were already about to release another single, 'Don't Knock The Rock', coupled with another album track, 'Choo Choo Ch' Boogie' (30148). Ironically, whilst 'Rudy's Rock' would remain on chart until February, 'Don't Knock The Rock', a song defending the teenagers' music, became the first Haley single not to reach the Top 100; but yet again, underscoring the disparity of markets, it would go Top Ten in Britain.

We have far less information on Haley's current nationwide tour, unlike the earlier, because this time he didn't keep a diary. Out on the road, he was not your typical boozing and womanising rock star. On the contrary, he laid down firm rules. The Comets, all married except Pompilii, were permitted no latitude either, despite the presence of groupies. Hotel room checks were not unknown, Pompilii was with Haley on this: 'If I wanted a chick I'd pay for one. Look, we're the number one act in the world. All we need is one guy in trouble with some young chick and there goes the act.' And if anyone was found talking to a fan with alcohol on their breath, they would find their job on the line. We may find Haley's stance on booze ironic, given later developments. British leader Vic Lewis had worked with Haley in the States and was struck by another feature: extravagance. He saw that on every show The Comets seemed to be in a different suit, 'Pastel blues or pinks, Scottish plaids, I just can't remember the whole range', he wrote in the *NME*. Such a wardrobe was clearly expensive to maintain, not to mention its transportation and other costs. And Haley seemed to need an 'entourage' with him when he was touring, bringing along his regional publishing representatives, their wives, their pals or whomever, all of whose travelling and hotel expenses were paid for by the singer. All this served no practical value: but the profoundly insecure Haley needed a lot of familiar faces around him when far from home, and it was costing him a bomb. All this would have consequences.

Notwithstanding the booze and women strictures, the Haley crew smoked heavily and swore – these were after all veterans of playing dives or army service – but within earshot of family and outsiders the language was toned down. Haley was protective of family and of children in general, which is why he was concerned about them being scorned for embracing rock'n'roll. Moreover, Haley's ego was heavily invested in the music, for he knew that if anyone could lay claim to starting it, it was he;; and because of this he felt personally responsible for the rumpus it had caused. Despite its rebellious tone Haley saw R&R as a harmless outlet for teenage energy. He was right, of course, but he was also acutely aware that whom the press really wanted to nail was not so much the kids as the music's protagonists. Eventually they would get Lewis and Freed, though these two almost went out of their way to get nailed. Hence Haley's concern with probity. He was not happy about Presley's 'suggestive' act and he must have winced at Presley's restoration of the original saucy lines in his version of 'Shake, Rattle And Roll'. Presley's antics could lead to an even greater backlash against the music which Haley feared would harm everyone. To some, Haley was the villain whose music paved the way for Presley, but this was never the case. Haley or no Haley, Presley would have happened. And neither would Presley be his undoing: Haley managed to achieve this all by himself.

The only other detail we have of Haley's final major tour of 1956 was a mid-November report in *Cash Box*: 'Despite a blinding 8-hour snow storm, it was "Standing Room Only" when Haley's package played Denver.'

November 10 in Britain, Haley had four singles in the Top Thirty, including new entry 'Rip It Up' at 21. More remarkable was the new entry at 30 of the LP, 'Rock'n'Roll Stage Show'. An album selling as quickly as a single was unheard of in those days, LPs being an indulgence unaffordable to most, particularly youngsters. The next week, 'Rip It Up' shot to No. 6. In December, it was No. 4 for two weeks, overwhelming the Little Richard disc which got no further than 30.

Haley closed the year with his traditional great Christmas party with all The Comets and their families. It is a nice touch that all their children knew one another and perhaps also went to the same schools. At Christmas, Haley was at his happiest, surrounded by family and friends; but his happiness was tinged with continuing regret at being separated from them. The season brought other regrets. Not only had he lost mother and father, he had lost a child and now also his sister: all effectively, one one way or another, premature deaths. None of his nuclear family were left, a circumstance which parallelled his spectacular success, underscoring his belief in divine retribution. Having arraigned deity against himself, no wonder he was doomed.

1956 had been a great year for him: two and a half years of hits with Decca had culminated with him becoming the biggest selling act of all time in Britain, where excitement was building at the prospect of a tour. Then there were the hit films and his continued headlining of sell-out package tours. 1957 looked extremely promising, but it was to be a year of surprises, surprises for which he was unprepared.

Watch them Climb!
TEN LITTLE INDIANS

Orchestrations printing
Song copy 1/6d.
MILLS MUS
MILLS HOUSE, DENMAR
COV 17

Rock 'n Roll Stage S

BILL HALEY
and his comets

(Above)
**Bill and The Comets
1954, clockwise:
Dick Richards,
Marshall Lyttle,
Joey Ambrose,
Johnny Grande,
Billy Williamson
and Bill**

Brunswick

R/T
56568
05616

RUDY'S ROCK
(Bill Haley, Rudy Pompilli)
BILL HALEY AND
HIS COMETS

**Bill and The Comets in Mid– 1958
Rudy Pompilli, Al Rex, Johnny
Grande, Ralph Jones,
Billy Williamson, Frank Beecher
and Bill.**

The Blackboard Jungle
(Richard Brooks, 1955, 101 m)

Cast: Glenn Ford, Anne Francis, Louis Calhern, Sidney Poitier.

A teacher strives to gain the respect of his pupils at a New York slum school. Diluted adaptation of Evan Hunter's novel but a significant movie – it was the first to feature rock music, Bill Haley's 'Rock Around The Clock' being utilized to great dramatic effect behind the film's opening credits. Public reaction was such that Columbia Pictures promptly signed up Haley to star in *Rock Around The Clock*. The rest, as they say, is history.

Rudy and Bill in 'Rock Around The Clock'

Daily Mirror

2d FORWARD WITH THE PEOPLE

HOW THE MIRROR BROUGHT THE KING OF ROCK 'N' ROLL TO HEP-HEP-HAPPY LONDON

FANTABULOUS!!

BILL HALEY'S OWN STORY of The welcome of my life!

EXCLUSIVE .... PAGE 2

In London with band leader Vic Lewis

BILL HALEY
Skinny Minnie; How Many
(Brunswick 05742) ★★

BILL Haley tries again with a growling, twanging slow pounder called **Skinny Minnie**. Personally I cannot see this one reaching any great heights—it's slow without much purpose.

Haley takes the vocal himself but the whole thing lacks vitality.

When he turns to **How Many** Haley sings again. And again it's a slow item. Not such a pounder as the one upstairs but another offering which has a casual, lazy feeling about it. One gets the impression, right or wrong, that Bill is looking anxiously for the way back.

I don't think this is it.

BILL HALEY
Lean Jean; Don't Nobody Move
(Brunswick 05752) ★★

IN the Skinny Minnie D Lizzy cut comes **Lean Jean** which Haley strikes out for a turn to favour.

A beater that paddles a fairly monotonously, it lacks frantic appeal of early Haley si but there's a certain amount compulsion. Bill himself han the lyric in which the humo just about as crude as you can

Don't Nobody Move is a quic beat item with a hesitation mick. I get the impression that this is so mechanical to Haley n

Bill joins in a song with British songstress Alma Cogan in Glasgow (photo c/o Spencer Leigh)

BILL HALEY
Joey's Song; Ooh! Look-a There, Ain't She Pretty
(Brunswick O5810) ★★★

NEW try from Bill Haley and his Comets comes with **Joey's Song**, which I find oddly attractive despite the somewhat dated feel about it. Not a wild rocker but a tuneful Latin beater using the rhythm and the sax simply and quite melodiously. Tune's quickly into your ear and the side may grow on plenty of people. No vocal.

There is a vocal from Bill on the flip, however. He husks a steady shuffler as if he were a new Louis Prima. Amusing and not unpleasant, but average fare only.

BILL HALEY AND HIS COMETS
(We're Gonna) Rock Around The Clock; Thirteen Women (Brunswick 05317).

THE first rock disc is revived by Brunswick and although it was made ten years ago it still sounds fresh. For anyone who has never heard this version, it's a punchy fast-moving compulsive rocker, good lyrics, excellent backing, and a tremendous beat. The sound is a little thin compared with some of todays recordings, but this is made up for in the tremendous atmosphere. Flip is a slower almost country type ballad.

TOP FIFTY TIP

Brunswick
45 RPM RECORDS

Bill Haley
SKOKIAAN
45-05818

SYNCOPATED R 'N' R

BILL HALEY
" Skokiaan "
" Puerto Rican Peddler "
(BRUNSWICK Q 5818)
★★★

GIVEN A CATCHY, syncopated R & R. setting, the old favourite " Skokiaan " comes over well in this new waxing by The Comets. Strictly instrumental, the melody is handled by the sax while the rest fill in the rhythm pattern.

With a Latin flavour, " Puerto Rican Peddler " is a pretty ditty given a treatment one scarcely anticipates from Mr. " Rock Around the Clock." The limited time goes through some key changes in this instrumental rendering. Pleasant.

BILL HALEY
I Got A Woman; Charmaine
(Brunswick O5788) ★★★★★

I GOT A Woman is the old Ray Charles success and it's really punched out by Haley, who might find himself back on the lists as a result.

His best beat half for ages, it has zip and an ear-grabbing. slapping noise from The Comets in the tight-sounding accompaniment. You can't write off Haley when he turns up with a half like this.

Poor old **Charmaine** never gets any rest does she ? Here she comes again, but Haley and the Comets treat her gently. They put a quiet, sentimental beat into the famous ballad and a lot of folk who always liked the song will still like it in this costume.

HAPPY BABY Bill Haley & His Comets   05910   Brunswick

THIS DISC MAY BRING BILL HALEY BACK

BILL HALEY
Mary Mary Lou; It's A Sin
(Brunswick 05735) ★★★★
D.N.T.

BILL HALEY pops up again, this time with a trip to hillbilly country. You'll find something of the country style on both halves here.

Mary Mary Lou is a bright rouser with a happy driving vocal from Haley himself—and the sax makes itself heard of course.

For the turnover Bill has even more of the country cut. **It's a Sin** makes a very effective coupling. Opens with la-la-la male group before Bill takes over the vocal again. A disc which could easily bring Bill back to the high rungs on the sales ladder. Watch it.

BILL HALEY ENTERTAINS THE DISC JOCKEYS

ROCK 'N' ROLL KING BILL HALEY laid on a special reception for British disc jockeys at the Savoy Hotel, London, W., on Monday. He wanted to meet them all personally, to thank and have a drink with them for their "kindness in taking such an interest in me." Bill, a very pleasant, unassuming fellow, told a RECORD MIRROR reporter that his current British tour was "the biggest thrill I have experienced in all my show business career."

In the picture are executives of the DECCA Record Company for which Bill Haley has set up record sales in this country. Left to right: BOB CRABB (exploitation); JIM FERGUSSON (Haley's manager); BILL HALEY; S. A. BEECHER - STEVENS (Sales Manager), and TONY HALL (exploitation Brunswick and Vogue-Coral labels).
—R.M. Picture.

JUNE THORBURN, pretty Rank star of 'True as a Turtle', now at the Leiceste Theatre, London, is also a rock 'n' roll fan and, of course, of BILL HALEY, whom back-stage during his recent London appearance. The two stars are pictured above

WILL HALEY COME BACK?

(I say – NO!)

by IAN DOVE

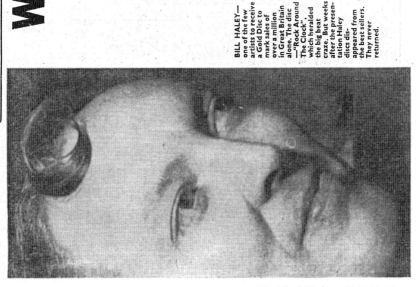

BILL HALEY— one of the few artists to receive a Gold Disc to mark sales of over a million in Great Britain alone. The disc "Rock Around The Clock", which heralded the big beat craze. But weeks after the presentation Haley discs disappeared from the best sellers. They never returned.

THE saddest people on the popular music scene today are the BILL HALEY fans.

For no artist has fallen so far and so fast as the deposed king of Rock 'n' roll, Bill Haley.

An EP just issued by Warner Bros., "Haley's Juke Box"—all fairly current Haley material—gives us an opportunity to judge Bill Haley in the light of present-day trends.

I must confess that if Haley hasn't changed I find it difficult to see just what the fuss was about back in the far-off days of late 1956 and 1957.

To be honest, about half the disc isn't rock 'n' roll and appears to be a peculiar mixture of rock and country and western. Net result, dullness.

"Wild Side of Life" is straight C & W and only "Detour" brings back the old Bill Haley. At least it brings back the style . . . but not the spirit.

● SET FOR YEARS

To those remembering Bill Haley of four years ago, this EP (Warner Bros. WEP 6025) must fill them with wonder and a slight sadness.

More than ever, I'm conscious of the quick changing world of show business.

Bill Haley's manager, Jolly Joyce, said in March, 1957, "He's set for years."

An EP just issued by Warner Bros., "Haley's Juke Box," —an opportunity to judge Bill Haley.

Months later Bill Haley was a stranger to Britain's best-selling charts.

They still can't find out what killed the goose that laid the golden discs. Why did the name Haley become unfashionable ?

Reasons aplenty are proffered. He didn't push his personality hard enough on stage. Prices for his British tour were too high. Supporting acts were too low standard and antagonised the fans.

Then there was the emerging of ELVIS PRESLEY — at the time a sideburned mystic from Memphis. Elvis was dubbed "sexy" on the grounds of his hip swivel. Everybody loved him.

And Bill Haley, short, tubby, with a cute kiss curl, was a different kettle of personality. A father figure, said the psychologists.

I don't honestly know what caused it. Maybe it was a combination of all these things. And it's a combination that this new EP will not help to unlock.

Warner Bros. don't turn out many singles at all, preferring only the dead cert. chart entrants like the Everly Bros. So it doesn't look like we are getting—at present—any of the reasonably successful Haley singles ("Let the Good Times Roll, Creole"), for example, issued in America.

● MILITANT FANS

But back to the fans . . . Apart from being the saddest, I'd say that they are the most militant. Roy Lister, manager of Warner Bros., for instance, has written to Haley Fan Club president, Fred Jackson, asking him to call them off.

And the Haley fans bitterly criticise the make-up of "Haley's Juke Box."

Vice-president Hugh McCallum says : "I believe Warner Bros. would be better off if they issued Bill's singles as EPs even at the expense of not issuing any items from American LPs.

"By releasing 'Chick Safari', 'Hawk', 'Let the Good Times Roll, Creole', 'So Right Tonight' on an EP, they would, I'm sure, derive more financial gain . . . than they will from either this 'Juke Box' EP or the first 'Bill Haley' EP."

But it's all really summed up, as far as I'm concerned on the EP's sleeve, which has the sub-title "Songs of the Bill Haley Generation."

And this isn't that generation.

THE HALEY DEBATE

Haley's 'Juke Box'

Sir,—I would like to thank Ian Dove for mentioning the Bill Haley "Juke Box" EP last week. I think Bill and the Comets have done the right thing by abandoning the old rock'n'roll band wagon to try something different.

The trend today is, I think, away from rock'n'roll towards experimenting with different sounds (as with the John Barry Seven and the Shadows) as well as the usual moon and June drivel.

If Bill Haley decides to continue to widen his musical scope by experimentation then that is OK by me—and I'm sure by Bill's millions of other fans.

And if Bill does a little idea-snatching sometimes I don't think it will matter. Lots of other stars (some are now top artists) have taken some of Haley's ideas. — GRAHAM N. RIGBY, 207, Kingsley Avenue, Kettering.

Not Commercial

Sir,—How can Ian Dove possibly base Bill Haley's chances of a come-back on the strength of Haley's "Juke Box" EP?

This disc is strictly for the fans and, as such, I think Warner Bros. made a big mistake in bothering to release it here at all. Most of the remaining Haley fans will certainly go the whole way and buy the LP of the same name from the States.

C & W enthusiasts may go for these offerings by Bill, but they are most certainly no indication of Haley at his commercial best.—SANDY SIMPSON, 53 Coulardhill, Lossiemouth, Morayshire.

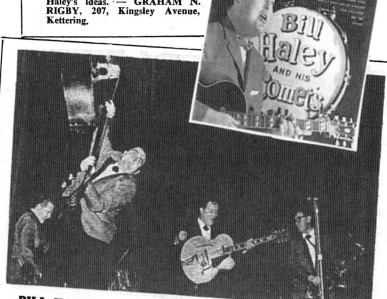

BILL HALEY & HIS COMETS—up to their stage antics.

I USED to think that Carl Perkins' "Blue Suede Shoes" was one of the greatest original rock numbers. Then I bought Bill Haley's "Rock The Joint" LP, most of which tracks were recorded in 1953. And "Whatcha Gonna Do," a Haley original, is almost exactly similar to "Blue Suede Shoes," even the opening chant. I'm afraid it proves, for me that Perkins was not such an original performer after all.—T. T. Laverick, 79 Broadway West, Gosforth, Newcastle-upon-Tyne.

KINDA CORNY

BILL HALEY

"*Tamiami*"
"*Candy Kisses*"

(WARNER BROTHERS WB 6)

★★★ IN A SLIGHTLY "corny"
kick, Billy's boys bounce
around "Tamiami" enthusi-
astically. A barroom piano
brightly shares honours with
the sax while the rest of the
Comets equally eagerly join in
the party.

Another C & W favourite that
has been on more than one best-
sellers chart, "Candy Kisses" is
returned to the C & W shelf
whence it came by Mr. Haley.
Bill's earliest days are recalled in
this strictly C & W vocal job he
turns in, while the rest of the
group play "sweet-corn".

BILL HALEY AND HIS COMETS
Rock Around The Clock; Love
Letters In The Sand (Warner Bros
WB 133).

THIS is the up-dated version of
the great hit. It's brisk and
slick and features a better
all-round sound than the hit. But
the atmosphere that made the 1954
disc sell fourteen million copies is
lacking. Flip is a good version of
the old Pat Boone hit. The disc
should make the charts on interest
appeal.

Bill Haley Label Switch
Jolly Joyce Again At Helm

FIRST stages in a big international comeback bid by **BILL HALEY** and
the COMETS has started in America with the news that the group have
returned to their former manager, **JOLLY JOYCE**, who was responsible for
their early hit parade triumphs.

Joyce's first move was to get the
Comets released from their contract
with **Warner Brothers Records** so that
they could sign with **Gone Records**, a
set-up owned by **George Goldner**

Says Joyce: "The boys will cut their
first sides some time this week and the
release dates won't be far behind. This
new disc contract is, I think, vital because it enables Bill to select his own
material for recording.

"Bill has a stack of worthwhile
numbers in preparation, though we
can't say too much about likely selec-
tions at this time."

Bill Haley has complained in the
past of being "sidetracked" on what
he considers the best material to get his
name back in the charts. The Comets
recently completed a successful season
in a night club in Somers Point, New
Jersey.

Bill Haley

Rock Around The Clock; Love Letters In The Sand (Warner Bros WB 133) ★★★★

NO, not a new version of Haley's old hit, but a version that's new to us. Made four years back this beater by Bill and the Comets uses all the group voices at start before Bill steps in with his familiar style. Noise is edgier than on the first Brunswick presentation and seems to use much more guitar. Bill thinks this is the better one—I'm not sure.

Love Letters In The Sand eases along in Hawaiian fashion.

BILL HALEY & HIS COMETS—up to their stage antics.

Bill and The Comets on ITV's 'Thank Your Lucky Stars' (Photo: ATV)

BILL HALEY (RM Pic)

The second gig of the opening night of Bill's '68 UK tour at the Victoria Ballroom, Chesterfield, Monday, April 29th., 1968 (Photos: John Firminger)

BILL HALEY and the Comets

The great leap
Backwards!

BILL Haley and the Comets did not perform an encore at the Royal Albert Hall because they were chased off stage by a mob of rockers. Earlier in the show, Duane Eddy's drummer had been hit on the head by a carefully-aimed bottle, stopping the rock for some minutes. And one of the go-go girl dancers employed to writhe on stage to the twangy guitar, had been the victim of a scratch-and-claw attack by a rocker girl.

Not only is this 1968, a year after the Beatles' "Sgt. Pepper", and 17 years after "Rock Around The Clock" was written, but the artistes who provoked this frenzy were mostly un-sexy American musicians. If you were not there, be assured that the sight of Bill Haley and his Comets being chased off stage by a group of people who at best looked like 1954 hippies was quite amusing. And the kids weren't the original beat generation, being nostalgic, who grew up with James Dean, the Suez Crisis, and 14 inch bottoms, but a strange breed of throwbacks, dedicated (or so it seems) to preserving the more ridiculous aspects of rock 'n' roll.

CURIOSITY AND NOSTALGIA

Most of the audience, though, had arrived at the Albert Hall because of a mixture of curiosity and nostalgia. Like me. And even the Quotations, who efficiently backed Duane Eddy were given more applause than boos when they attempted—not too solidly—to reproduce those dear dead rock sounds. Another group called "The Wild Angels" obviously had their hearts more in rock, as could be seen from their attire and hair, a fact which was appreciatively reflected by the hot, excited multitude around the stage.

During Duane Eddy's rendition of the monotonous, but primitive jungle tune "Peter Gunn" the rockers around the stage were so frenzied that I imagined the whole stage, noise and writhing multitude, sinking into the fires of iniquity below, the floor of the Albert Hall being split asunder by an unseen, righteous and wrathful hand. Duane's fine guitar work has never been truly showcased on his hit singles and he only had time to perform a few of them, all of which followed the same twangy guitar, sax and percussion format. Duane looked as though he was waiting at a bus stop, not playing to a hotbed of rock revivalism, and his coolness carried him through well.

Haley, of course, was excellent. His sound is much stronger than on those early records of his, and his showmanship, sheer professionalism and ability to lay down a real beat created a tremendous atmosphere with everybody.

THE FULL CYCLE

"I want to tell you all," said Bill, "How very happy you've made me tonight."

Bill made everyone else happy too.

But he did insist before he came on that no one gets on the stage. "I knew rock and roll would come back, it's gone the full cycle," he said.

Even to the riots it seems. But for those Bill isn't responsible, of course. But what he is responsible for, good or bad, is something you realise when you see him singing "Rock Around The Clock". Namely, that pop music would never have been the multi-million pound industry it is today, employing hundreds of thousands of people (including me) and giving pleasure, misguided or not, to literally millions of young people. I'm just glad that there are pop fans who want to advance themselves musically and culturally to more satisfying things, to offset the others who would like to return to the days of violence, repetition and the big beat: after all, those magic, exciting sounds of the fifties can never again be copied or imitated successfully because this is 1968.

NORMAN JOPLING

BILL HALEY
Spanish Twist; My Kind Of Woman ★★★★
(London HLU 9471)

WELL, well, well! It is April, 1960, since Haley had his previous single released in this country. He comes fighting back with an attempt to join the Twist trend.

Up Bill's street, of course. His group rock professionally and quite contagiously. Haley himself husks out the vocal. Be very interesting to note reactions from the public and to see if the Comets are due for a rise again. **Spanish Twist** could be the re-start of something.

My Kind Of Woman is a thumping, raucous rocker which has Haley chanting the vocal again.

Bill Haley: 'Now we're part of pop history!'

Bill Haley: Violence in Britain

BILL HALEY and the Comets are back in town, hot, or rather cold from a Scandinavian tour that ended with a midnight concert in Lapland, with the sun still shining and the temperature at ten degrees below freezing!

"I was so cold I couldn't even feel my fingers," said smiling Bill, resplendent in summer tan and dark glasses and looking as far removed from everyman's impression of a hardened rocker as ever.

Bill's here for some six weeks, during which he's playing his first-ever cabaret dates in his 15-year history. This week it's Stockton Fiesta and Middlesbrough Excel, next week Manchester Broadway and Talk Of The North, and August 3 week at Whalley Ace Of Clubs and Stockport Baa Baa.

Then there's a week in Germany and back to Britain at the end of August for a proposed tour of Mecca Ballrooms and the possibility of a London free open-air concert in any park that will take him.

But wherever Bill goes in England, the rockers follow, and the inevitable violence.

"I know this is the image I've got, and it's always been a great problem for us.

"I don't know why it is but this violent minority only shows itself in Britain. There's never been any trouble anywhere else in the world.

"It may just be an ex-change between the older fans who knew me when I started and the younger fans. And, quite honestly, I can't think of any way of stopping it. They are loyal, this violent minority, and you can't stop them from coming to concerts."

But Bill and the Comets are shrewd nuts. They know that without the excitements on and off stage at his concerts, the papers are immediately going to pronounce him dead.

"Anyway, what happened at the Albert Hall last year was child's play compared to some of the scenes we've experienced along the road."

It's been a long road for Bill, Rudi Pompelli and the others. How have they lasted so long and why are they all still together, almost like a grand old family of rocking grandfathers?

"I know it's going to sound terribly corny, but somehow we feel like historians. We were the originators of rock-n-roll in the early fifties and rock-n-roll changed the entire concept of popular music.

"So we feel it's right we should still be playing this music to the kids—audiences who never saw us first time round—just to prove to them that we invented the music and here we are still playing it.

"Without us around no one is going to be able to see how it all began. It's a case of being part of the history of music."

So what of Bill Haley, cabaret artist?

"Even I don't know what we'll be doing yet," he said on Monday, just before boarding the train to Stockton. "But I hope these next few weeks will give us a chance to do some things we've not done for a long time. I'd like to include some guitar solos, Rudi playing things like "Harlem Nocturn," and even a few country and western numbers.

"And of course, 'Rock Around The Clock.' Every night I say a little prayer for 'Rock Around The Clock'—without it I'd be a nobody."

HALEY & THE COMETS "ROCK AROUND THE ⟨COU⟩NTRY"*** Sonet SNTF 623
Side 1: Dance Around The Clock/Games People Play/ A Little Piece At A Time/I Wouldn't Have Missed It For The World/Bony Maronie/There's A New Moon Over My Shoulder
Side Two: Me And Bobby McGee/How Many/Who'll Stop The Rain/Pink Eyed Pussycat/Travelin' Band/No Letter Today

⟨A⟩nother one time ex-big popper comes back to the Country, ⟨a⟩lthough in this case Bill has made the whole trip, Per-⟨s⟩onally I enjoyed quite a few of the tracks. The title is ⟨s⟩ort of a Country rock version of his song that caused ⟨a⟩ll the trouble years ago. Bill recorded this for a Scandin-⟨a⟩vian Company, in Nashville. Standout on the album is the ⟨s⟩uperb steel playing of Curley Chalker, the steelies' steel ⟨p⟩layer. They twice spelt his name wrong on this record, ⟨m⟩aybe they don't realise who he is but I know many steel fans ⟨w⟩ho will get his record for one reason. Bill messes up ⟨'⟩Games People Play' but does a great job on 'How Many' ⟨w⟩here Chalker comes to the fore. Also on the session were ⟨J⟩immie Riddle, 'Pig' Robbins and lead guitarist Nick Masters, ⟨H⟩aley's travelling lead man who sings on 'Travelling Band'. ⟨L⟩isten first but you might well find it infectious. I did.

Everybody Razzle Dazzle, Bill on stage in Middlesbrough, July 1969

5. Overseas

The new year began with his first tours overseas, Australia and the UK. Already, on Tuesday, January 1 at 11.00 a.m., he was on the plane to Detroit; but instead of excitement he felt trepidation, for he faced the longest flight of his life across the Pacific and the discomforting thought of lengthy flights across the Australian continent. His fear of flying was public knowledge and he usually preferred long car and train rides to the aeroplane, even when the latter took a fraction of the time, which must have exasperated some of his travelling companions. Both the Australian and British tours are well documented, so I will confine myself to a brief account. It was the first time either country had seen an American rock'n'roll show. The Australians got a much better deal than the British, for Haley headlined a show that featured Freddie Bell and The Bell Boys, The Platters, Big Joe Turner and LaVern Baker. Haley's fee was an astonishing $77,000 and the tour broke all Australian box office records. In three weeks, the ensemble played to 330,000 people, with many thousands more turned away. In Sydney alone, the show played to 86,000 in seven performances. The tour proved a good exercise in public relations for rock'n'roll, for audiences everywhere were well behaved, nailing the lie that the music equalled trouble and riots. Tremendously positive press coverage forced those radio stations who previously wouldn't play R&R to lift their ban. Yet Haley remained a troubled man. His immune system weakened by climate changes, jet lag and anxiety, he developed a fever and a very sore throat. Yet he didn't miss a show, perhaps only made possible because the band shared vocals, at this critical juncture an extremely good idea. One of the country's leading throat specialists was flown in to treat the singer and within a week he was much better. A conflicting report suggests that he did miss some shows, setting him back a cool $30,000.

During the day, when the others were out enjoying themselves, he would remain marooned in his hotel suite, drinking endless ('40 cups of') coffee, dwelling on his private losses against his public gains, nerves wracked at the thought of never ending long distance flights, pining for wife and family and running up gargantuan phone bills. He took comfort in the thought of soon returning home, albeit for only two days, and then onward to England with Cuppy – not by plane, but in the luxurious ambience of the *Queen Elizabeth*. Haley, a yachtsman, enjoyed the prospect of an unhurried sea voyage. But Australian promoter Lee Gordon had other ideas. He desperately wanted the singer to do another week and made him a fabulous offer: $100,000 under the table and payment of everyone's air fares to England, in addition to flying Cuppy from Philadephia to London, and the other Comets' wives too. Haley turned him down and did himself no favours. The return flight across the Pacific was a nightmare – the plane went through a monsoon – and landed in the middle of a snow storm in San Francisco (Monday, January 28), followed by another rough flight to New York. January 31, the 17 members of the Haley entourage (which included Ferguson and his mother, Jolly Joyce and his wife – and all this paid for out of Haley's pocket at London's swank Savoy Hotel!) boarded the luxury liner for what they thought would be a very pleasurable crossing of the Atlantic. After two days, the ship was caught in a hurricane: almost everyone was violently seasick. Given his bad luck in travelling, Haley doubtless also interpreted this as some kind of sign of the Almighty's displeasure.

In Britain, January had been a month of heightened anticipation of Haley's visit, fuelled largely by the *Daily Mirror* and the *NME*. Articles by the singer, ghost-written by staff writers, appeared frequently, and make amusing reading when compared to his true feelings. 'I can't wait to get to England', 'I'm dying to meet my fans in the UK', and so on. The three-week tour was already a sell-out, fans queueing in the cold night for twelve hours waiting for the morning box office to open, chanting 'See You Later, Alligator' and 'Shake, Rattle And Roll' to pass the time. Even before Haley had set foot in the country, promoters Lew and Leslie Grade were negotiating for the singer to do a further 12 dates. When the liner docked at Southampton on Wednesday, February 6 at 2.00 p.m., all hell broke loose. Thousands of fans were waiting and the Haley entourage was literally under siege as mobs broke through the police cordon, surrounding and climbing all over the cars on hand to take them to the train. The singer got separated from his wife, she marooned in another car, terrified and in tears as the horde trapped the vehicle. Haley's clothes were torn and at one point he had to be carried – literally – by police to safety. When the *Daily Mirror*'s sponsored *Rock'n'Roll Express* – on which were several hundred fans travelling to meet their idols, organised by the paper – arrived at London's Waterloo in the rush hour, the station was brought to a stop by an estimated 4000 fans. The Pathe newsreel showed a charismatic, smiling Haley negotiating the melée – outwardly always the professional – but inwardly he must have been petrified. The latest *NME* chart data, disclosed to Haley then, but published three days later (February 9), showed 'Don't Knock The Rock' leaping in at No. 15 as the film went on general release as a 'B' feature; 'Rip It Up' climbing back up to 14, and 'Rock The Joint', the 1952 Essex recording, issued on London-American, at 21. 'Rock Around The Clock' had just vacated the chart after achieving a million in UK sales and Haley was awarded a gold disc at a Decca-Brunswick reception for the singer at London's Savoy. World sales of the record had now exceeded six million, making it the biggest selling record of the decade. But little of this assuaged Haley's anxiety about his personal safety, an anxiety which now extended to the mother of his children, not to mention The Comets' wives. The scenes at Southampton and Waterloo were a direct consequence of the Grades' advance promotion with the press. So public was Haley's arrival that fans were positioned along the track-side waving at the train! Haley and Ferguson held the promoters responsible for the mob fiascos and threatened to return to the States at once. The Grades' response was unprecedented security for the entourage. Even the women's shopping sprees were not allowed without security guards. On one occasion, Cuppy and Mary Rex, Al's wife, sneaked out of the Savoy without a guard and got no further than the Charing Cross Road when fans accosted them. Everywhere the entourage went, fans were present, frequently in hordes: at hotels, back stage doors, etc. 3000 were waiting when Haley alighted from the train at Glasgow. They wanted a piece of any Comet, let alone Haley. Some must have thought they had got Elvis too when they saw Comets' 'band boy' Vince 'Catfish' Broomall, an absolutely cool looking 18-year old with a Presley appearance.

The tour passed without violence. There was no repeat of the mayhem that attended the screenings of 'Rock Around The Clock': no dancing in the aisles or storming of the stage, fans beside themselves had to make do with gyrating in their seats, for the theatre 'heavies' were ubiquitous. The Grades had made good their commitment to Haley's security: but they had their own beef with the singer. Watching the act at London's Dominion, they were dismayed it lasted only 30 minutes. This was standard practice in the US, where Haley headlined shows consisting of many other acts with ten–fifteen minute spots. But in Britain, rock-hungry audiences had to endure one hour of the Vic Lewis Orchestra and 'family' acts about which they couldn't care less, before seeing the act for which they had paid good money. And Haley wouldn't give encores. Audiences would stand, stamp and shout for more, even through the National Anthem, but still Haley wouldn't come out. By all accounts, the shows were electrifying, yet anti-climactic for their brevity. Audiences were a sight: rows and rows of Teddy Boys, girls in long, tight black skirts or in blue, red or yellow jeans. Music critics, hardly sympathetic to rock'n'roll, were appalled at the din The Comets made and bemused by Haley, the most amusing comments describing him as looking like 'a genial butcher' and that he had 'an innocent, greedy look, slipping his tongue around in his mouth and looking upward with boyish eyes, like a fat boy eyeing a huge ice cream'. Haley extended the act to 45 minutes, but many still felt short-changed. The additional twelve dates were not all sell-outs. Two dates in Dublin were attended by mob scenes; but the following two dates at Belfast's Hippodrome saw the house only half to three-quarters full. In Northern Ireland, a moral climate not unlike America's Deep South prevailed, rock'n'roll was fiercely frowned upon as 'animalistic' and 'immoral' and Haley's films were banned.

The tour finished on March 10 at the Dominion where it had begun 4½ weeks earlier. It had been Haley's most intensive, which permitted no TV or radio work, and he had not one single day off. He did two shows nightly and matinees on Saturdays and sometimes on Sunday. It was at a matinee in Kilburn (north-west London – Sunday, 24th) that he first noted a house that was not packed. His brief diary entries are our only glimpses into the thinking of this most private man. Despite nerves and fatigue, it was clear that he did not like it at all when he saw empty seats, even though in the case of Britain it made no difference to his income (unlike in the States where he took a percentage of ticket sales). So when he returned to Waterloo for the first leg of his trip home, he must have been alarmed that only a small band of fans were there to see him off. No crowds, no mobs: the effect must have been eerie when compared to the scenes of his arrival – and unsettling. Likewise at Southampton, he left unnoticed.

What on earth had happened?

Nobody could have imagined this, least of all Haley himself. Changes were afoot. In the words of Chris Gardner, 'Haley's fall from popularity was one of the most sudden in the entire history of show business.' At this point his diary suddenly falls silent. According to *Cash Box*, half a million had seen Haley in the British Isles: even if we halve this number, that is a mighty sample of the teenage record-buying public. Yet, in the third week of the tour, 'Rip It Up' rose six places on *NME*'s list and in the week *after* his departure, 'Don't Knock The Rock' moved up by four.

Trying to fathom the mystery of Haley's fall is not easy. The usual explanations offered do not stand up to scrutiny. 'He was too old and lacked sexual charisma': but UK fans already knew that from his films, and neither did such considerations stop them from buying Fats Domino and Chuck Berry who would still enjoy hits years later; moreover, in the US, most kids realised that Alan Freed was old enough to be their dad, yet his ratings soared. 'Kids ditched him for the younger, more exciting Elvis.' No, they didn't., they made no more a 'choice' between Haley and Presley than they did with Little Richard and Gene Vincent and, later, Jerry Lee Lewis and Eddie Cochran.

In the US, Haley's fans had seen him over and over again during a five-year period, making him the highest paid act on the rock'n'roll circuit; yet he was bigger nowhere than in Britain, which made his overnight fall all the more startling. The brevity of his act is suggested as a contributory factor, yet Australian fans bought *more* of his records after his tour. The US trade got wind of the dissatisfaction in Britain and ventured an interesting thought: that youngsters' income was limited, so often they would have to choose between seeing the act or buying records. In the case of Haley, the choice was stark, for the cost of seeing him seemed excessive. And therein lies the rub. They had to pay more to see an act that delivered less. Certainly, some felt taken and thought twice about the next Haley record they considered buying, and if they had to choose between the latest Little Richard or Elvis Presley, the memory of being short-changed by Haley made the choice easier. Australian teenagers had higher incomes; in any event, they got a better show, getting not only Haley but also Joe Turner, LaVern Baker, and so on. Which made it perplexing why a British rock-hungry audience was offered an hour of the Vic Lewis Orchestra and co. before Haley. It was not fair to the entertainers and grievously unfair to the fans who had paid good money to see a R&R show. Did not Ferguson and Haley first consult with the Grades about the support acts? Or did they only care about the money, and as for the fans, 'Why should they complain – they're getting the American act they most want to see.' Because of the Musicians' Union, a support act of American rock'n'rollers could not come to the UK, but the Grades could have organised local talent: Tony Crombie and His Rockets, Tommy Steele, Rory Blackwell and The Blackjacks, for example.

Elsewhere, Haley's star continued to shine. Whilst he was in Britain, 'Rock Around The Clock' had been No. 1 in Italy, and 'See You Later Alligator' rose to

No. 14 on the German Top 50. No sooner was he back home than Milt Gabler drove down from New York to 'Melody Manor' to brief him on the next recording projects which had become a matter or urgency as the singer had been away so long. Haley apparently had a den at his home where he and The Comets would try out new arrangements. March 22, they were at the Pythian to record three sides, 'Miss You', and two tunes written by one J. Leslie MacFarland, '(You Hit The Wrong Note) Billy Goat' and 'Rockin', Rollin' Rover'. There then followed sessions on the 25th, 29th and April 3 for an album, 'Rockin' The Oldies', Haley's first suicidal project. Neither was the single 'Billy Goat'/'Rover' a clever idea, for after 13 consecutive cracking singles in three years, in one stroke he dived back into the corn of the Essex days. Presumably his thinking behind the 'Oldies' concept was that songs recognised by the teenagers' parents but set to a rockin' rhythm would make R&R less unacceptable to them. Or perhaps Haley, anxiety-ridden by the constant threat posed by over-zealous teenage fans, hoped that if the 'Oldies' idea worked it would pave the way to performing to more sedate audiences. What in fact transpired from these sessions was a collection of uninspired perform-ances which did nothing for the songs, songs which youngsters did not want and which made no impression on their parents who preferred to hear them performed by more melodic singers. Rockin' up standards was always a precarious practice, sometimes it worked – as in the case of Fats Domino – but more often it didn't. Two features peculiar to this second album were that Haley, unlike in the first, sang all songs himself – perhaps Gabler's reaction to criticism of the singer's absence on so many tracks previously – and the subdued quality of the tenor sax. Pompilii had taken ill and could not make all four sessions, his place being taken by one Frank Scott. At this time, Haley's last great single, for the present, '40 Cups Of Coffee' (backed with 'Hook, Line And Sinker' taken from the debut album, Decca 30214) made it into the Top 100, but went no further than 70, despite the act appearing on the hugely influential 'Ed Sullivan TV Show' (April 28). They were again on national TV on May 9, 'Roy Bolger's Washington Square Show', performing '(You Hit The Wrong Note) Billy Goat'. We may understand why they thought it was a good idea at the time, for they probably thought it could become a popular catch phrase like 'See You Later, Alligator', but that had cool and attitude, unlike 'Billy Goat' which was decidedly uncool and contrived. Even so, Decca 30314 sailed up to No. 60 on the record world's most coveted chart. This steady flow of modest national hits kept Haley's booking schedule for months ahead. A tour began at Mahoney, Pennsylvania, on May 11 and ended in Angola, Indiana, on June 2. The act then went to Jamaica, and June closed with dates in Maryland and Connecticut; in the latter they did an open air show at Bridgeport with the unlikely co-act being jazz giant Lionel Hampton; but still not as bizarre as coupling Haley with the Vic Lewis Orchestra.

July 15 produced a session of mixed quality. For the first time since 1952, Haley recorded a ballad, 'How Many?', though a few months earlier he had cut 'Miss You', which could have been classed as a ballad but for the tempo and arrangement. 'How Many?' is slow tempo and convincing evidence that the singer should have stuck to R&R. Heaven only knows what got into his head to record this: it is so far removed from what his public wanted or even expected. Perhaps he thought it could be pitched to the country market; but what was the point? He knew the country door was firmly shut in his face and, besides, that market was awash with far more convincing performances. The other two sides on this recording date were a different story altogether. Hank Williams' 'Move It On Over' had been a part of Haley's repertoire back in the 4 Aces Of Swing days and he must have been struck by its similarity to 'Rock Around The Clock'. It was therefore a natural for him to record and on this session he delivered it with gusto against Pompilii's driving sax riff and Beecher's blistering guitar. 'Rock The Joint' is similarly inspired. Recent recordings suggested Haley was losing his way, but he was definitely on the ball now. Given the trouble caused by the song's publishers over this song, it was a wonder he considered re-recording it at all. This was not merely a re-cut, but a thoroughly inventive and hip re-arrangement. Haley and Gabler must have thought they had a sure-fire hit on their hands here.

It has been said that Presley was Haley's nemesis. This, of course, is nonsense, for if anyone could have been said to have affected his status it was another southerner, a guy with a piano that it was said he 'pumped' rather than played, but in point of fact he actually *hammered* it. This was Jerry Lee Lewis who, on July 28, caused a sensation with his appearance on NBC-TV's nationally networked 'Steve Allen Show', when he kicked away his piano stool while performing 'Whole Lotta Shakin' Goin' On'. Here was a cat that made Presley look like Perry Como. Allen, to his credit, instead of fleeing the fuss, got this renegade back on his show within two weeks for another ratings-soaring appearance. In the next six months, Lewis would become as big in record sales as Presley was at the beginning of '56, which would have repercussions for Haley, who, despite his popularity, had not a Top Ten hit since then.

Through July and August, he did fewer shows than usual, preferring time with his family on his yacht. He would do a 9-to-5 routine at his Chester office, attending to his various publishing and business interests. To a man tired of life on the road and show-biz glitz, such sedentary work was necessary. Gigs were confined within the state, the most significant being a show with his boyhood idol, Gene Autry. Meanwhile, 'The Dipsy Doodle'/'Miss You' (30394) was released and was the second single not to reach the Top 100. August 30 for three days, he appeared at the Michigan State Fair; then a residency at the Casino Cafe in Sea Isle City., New Jersey, before a tour of the Mid-West which was to finish in Hollywood, where Haley was to begin shooting his third film with Alan Freed. This never materialised, so he continued touring the West Coast, ending on October 16. At this time, 'Rock The Joint'/'How Many?' (30461) was released and, remarkably, this, too, didn't make the 100.

Also issued about this time, and for which 'The Dipsy Doodle' and 'Miss You' paved the way, but apparently to no avail, was the album recorded in the Spring, 'Rockin' The Oldies' (8569). All of November was devoted to two projects, the rehearsal for and appearance on two TV shows, 'The Big Record Show' (15th) and 'American Bandstand (27th), and the recording of a third album. Twelve songs were recorded, and two for the next single, were recorded over five sessions. Haley's idea for the album was another suggesting that he was out of touch with teenagers' tastes. After the 'oldies' idea he now wanted to 'rock' ... international folk tunes, perhaps inspired by his status as an international act, of particular importance now that domestic sales were falling. It's the beginning of November and the American charts had Presley rockin' the jailhouse at No. 1, Ricky Nelson with his be-bop baby at 7, Little Richard knockin' at 10, Lewis still shakin' at 14 and Vincent offering a lotta lovin' at 18; and Haley believed that the kids would now go for 'London Bridge is falling down' and 'Waltzing Matilda'. Rusty Keefer, who had been one of the 4 Aces Of Western Swing in the early days, was in a publishing contract with the singer and was commissioned to put new lyrics to the traditional tunes. The songs show the composing credits of 'Haley-Gabler-Keefer-Cafra (Williamson)'; so Gabler was not only producing the act, but also now a part of it. The choice of songs would have been Haley's. Gabler suggested the appropriate adaptations and arrangements, Keefer did the words – he also played guitar on all five sessions, accompanying Beecher and Haley; Williamson's contribution is less clear but he was always an ideas' man and doubtless his credit is justified. 'Rockin' Around The World', as the album was called, did, however, have its moments. It had more charm and verve than the 'Oldies' and Haley seems more comfortable vocally. Vocally, he was absent only on 'Jamaica DJ' which Williamson sang with fun and gusto against a fiery rhythm. Williamson's mock English toff interjections on 'Piccadilly Rock' raise a smile, and perhaps not for the reason intended. The Comets' vocal gibberish on 'Me Rock-A-Hula' must have creased them up; and indeed if the album is listened to without prejudice and preconception, one can find a lot to enjoy. But surely merely 'to entertain' was not the point. Haley seemed to be relegating himself to a variety-comic role, perhaps in the belief that this was the way forward when the R&R boom went bust. This album and the previous certainly suggest that he was seeking to broaden his horizons but, as time would tell, he seriously miscalculated.

The Comets were also working on a separate project: a single by an old Haley friend, Lou Graham, a hillbilly singer who had worked as an announcer back in the WPWA days. At Haley's Chester studio, the combo backed Graham on 'Wee Willie Brown', a song written by Rex and Williamson; amusingly, Ferguson's name also appeared on the composing credits. This is an exciting R&R record, owing much to the tight, driving rhythm of the band and Beecher's sizzling guitar very much to the fore. What is extraordinary is why Haley didn't record this himself; but he was too busy recording 'Wooden Shoe Rock' and 'Rockin', Rollin' Schnitzelbank'. The record was cut for Clymax, a label functioning as an outlet for Haley's publishing interests; but there seems to be no evidence of its release under this imprint, and indeed it quickly appeared on Decca's Coral subsidiary (January 1958). The shadowy Clymax, and other reported Haley labels, may not have operated as such, existing only to facilitate in-house masters for lease to record companies.

6. Troubles

Haley's concern with publishing had become an obsession. In the music business then, as now, whomever owned the publishing made the money. But this obsession was to undo Haley. It led to his rift with James Myers. Myers, though always working with his own interests in mind – and there was nothing wrong with that – was a massively beneficial influence on Haley's career, and Haley managed to alienate him. It was Myers who got him the deal with Decca and a producer who maximised his potential, which would make him world famous and rich. Myers' price was that every single had to have one side, if not both, with his copyright. He didn't care who wrote the song – it could be one of his writers or Haley's – so long as he owned the publishing rights. Haley agreed and they shook hands on it. The singer honourably kept his promise but when three Comets left to become The Jodimars he began to see things differently. Myers got in with The Jodimars and their manager, Frank Pingatore, writer of two Haley hits. Despite appearances, Haley was aggrieved by The Comets' split, feeling betrayed not only by them but also by Pingatore and now Myers, with whom he felt no moral necessity to continue honouring his agreement, a man he had made very rich, for he turned otherwise worthless Myers' copyrights into money-spinners. But Myers kept his eye on the ball rather than injured pride. Despite the fall-out with the singer, he kept hustling for 'Rock Around The Clock' and Haley and managed to set up a fabulous deal with Desilu Productions – producers of the hit TV show, 'I Love Lucy' – worth a cool half a million dollars. The singer was to get his own nationally networked TV show of 39 weekly half-hour broadcasts at $10,000 each. Additionally, he would get $10,000 just for signing the contract plus 10% of any international revenue. What happened next is unclear, but it seems that the tentative title of the show was 'Rock Around The Clock With Bill Haley', featuring songs by Haley and the Comets, comedy sketches and guest artistes. Myers' interest was the inclusion of songs he owned. He was stunned when Haley's reaction to this heaven-sent deal was an emphatic 'no' to any song by Frank Pingatore and to any appearance by The Jodimars. I use the word 'heaven-sent' purposefully. Assuming there is no vital missing detail that would dramatically change our perception, Haley was, not to put too fine a point on it, a complete and bloody fool. Although in the top 50% tax bracket, he had failed to set aside funds for the inevitable annual tax bill, and *he failed to do so year after year*. Having squandered his fortune and with the Internal Revenue Service hot on his trail, one would have expected him to greet the Desilu deal with open arms instead of jeopardising it.

The singer's general attitude was also baffling. He enjoyed being feted for his popularity and his status as show headliner, yet loathed engaging with the people who made it all possible, be it record industry chiefs or simple fans. Up to his eyes in debt, he was yet preoccupied with appearance: everyone in his organisation had to run Cadillacs, for it had to be seen that whoever worked for Bill Haley was doing well. The man who had refused a pay rise to the former Comets financed pointless hangers-on to accompany him on tour. He acquired a reputation for initiating hare-brained business ventures and the word went around that cheques issued in his name were suspect. Simultaneous to needlessly squandering thousands of dollars, he was failing to keep up basic payments to his first wife and their child. He avoided mixing with the important people in the record and show business worlds, people whose influence could help his career. He thought he didn't need them; and it was such arrogance which kept his fees high, possibly with dire consequences in the UK where many perceived him as demanding so much for so little commensuration. He seemed to have been misled by his international success: not fully appreciating that being No. 4 in Italy and No. 70 in the US was a worrying trend: it needed to be the other way round.

Even more baffling is that this man – to whom home and family was everything – had now created the totally unnecessary situation of being *compelled* to tour more because of his tax bills. Generally, when an act is in trouble the fault can often be found in the management or in the record company, for an act's fate invariably depends on forces outside its control. Not so, Bill Haley. A seasoned performer in his early thirties, he was experienced in all aspects of the business: stagecraft, writing, arranging, publishing, distribution, promotion, leasing, radio, TV, the gauging and setting of fees. This was entirely unlike his contemporaries of the late fifties who were usually some ten years younger and with little or no experience of anything and frequently exploited ruthlessly by both management and record company. Haley, on the other hand, was very much in control and not manipulated by either manager or label. Whilst at other times he comes across as weak – fearful of crowds, needing others around him, and so on – he was strong in other areas. He called the shots, and he knew full well what a shyster Ferguson was. Ferguson was both incompetent and devious, evoking in others at best contempt and at worst, disgust. Apart from facilitating Haley's transition from country to pop – from Saddlemen to Comets – it is hard to see how his management was helpful. He was a no-talent with a gambling habit to support, whose dubious methods seemed to rub off on Haley, particularly in the vital matter of paying taxes. Haley's negligence was inexcusable, for over the years he would have heard so many times from others – particularly in the music business – the perils of not setting aside a portion of one's income for the taxman. For a man otherwise so cautious and conservative, Haley could be inexplicably irresponsible and reckless.

Gabler would let Haley record anything he wanted, but he had the final word on what was released. He felt Haley was short-changing himself, for he was refusing to record excellent material by black writers writing with him in mind. Everyone knew what wonders the Gabler-Haley partnership could achieve with black material, but the singer wouldn't consider it because he did not own a stake in the publishing, never mind the fact that there could be a million-selling tune in the offing. In Gabler's view, what he was turning down was far better than what Haley was recording, and he should know. Someone close to Haley at this time observed that he was the worst kind of fool, 'one that thought he was smart'. A strong song could give him the big hit he needed and if he didn't own the publishing, he could still do all right by having one of his own copyrights on the flip. Worse still, even when he did record an 'outside' song, Ferguson had the gall to phone the publishers during the actual session, threatening the song would not be released unless they had a piece of the publishing (this was nonsense, for Haley and Ferguson could not dictate to Decca what should or should not be released). Moreover, during the next two years, Gabler was to become more and more concerned about the Comets' lack of preparedness for recordings. Exhaustion and disorientation from endless touring were to take their toll and insufficient time was given to recording projects. Songs were rehearsed at the last minute and not enough thought was given to the arrangements. It does seem to be the case that acts who spend a lot of time in the studio and whose recorded output is prodigious seem to have more hits, whilst those who live on the road and rarely get into the studio are less successful.

1958 opened with the release of the seventeenth Decca single, 'Mary, Mary Lou'/'It's A Sin' (30530), recorded on November 19 during the 'Rockin' Around The World' sessions. The flip was a version of a 1947 hit and was Haley's third consecutive 'B' side ballad. One wonders at the thinking behind the possibility of launching Haley as a balladeer: over three years of double-sided dance records suddenly followed by three consecutive 'B' side ballads suggests that there was a strategy in place, a plan to take him to another audience. Gabler believed Haley lacked credibility as a country singer, for the artist's delivery was rooted in the hillbilly corn of earlier decades. Haley's ballads, despite the contemporary arrangements, were totally unsuited to the pop market, least of all the teenage: he clearly misread both his own talent and his audience. Gabler was hipper to the market: it was he who suggested the singer should record 'Mary, Mary Lou'. This bright infectious tune, whilst not exactly a rocker, was ideally suited to Haley's style. The song had already been a minor territorial success a few months earlier by a quintet, The Sparks, also on Decca, whose leader was the composer. Yet, despite the song's hit potential and Haley's fine recording, it was the singer's third consecutive single to fail to break nationally. But Haley still made money for Decca. In the previous twelve months, every one of his singles had made the Top Five in Italy, whilst his latest there, 'Razzle Dazzle' – his disc schedule there seemed to be about two years behind – was about to do the same. In addition to this impressive tally in the world's ninth largest market, in the second largest,. Britain, despite no appearances in the *NME* Top Thirty, every Haley release enjoyed good sales. So whilst he was no longer a big seller domestically he was still a sound investment for his record company.

'Mary, Mary Lou' was not lucky for Haley, but there is an interesting twist to the song's story. Sam Cooke – who interestingly enough met Haley about the time of his version – recorded the song in 1960 and it may have been his recording which made an impression on Gene Pitney. When the following year Rick Nelson had a million-seller with Pitney's composition 'Hello, Mary Lou', the publishers of 'Mary, Mary Lou' sued and obtained a 50% share of the song. On first hearing, both songs seem different, but hum them and you find yourself humming the same tune. 'Mary, Mary Lou' notwithstanding, Haley was about to get lucky anyway. It was February 6 at the Pythian and the Haley-Gabler-Keefer-Williamson combination had cooked up three songs based on three of the big hits of the day. In the current issue of *Billboard*, 'Bony Moronie' by Larry Williams was at No. 21, The Diamonds' 'The Stroll' was at 8, and at No. 1, Danny & The Juniors' 'At The Hop'. It was Gabler who suggested 'Skinny Minnie' after Williams' impossibly thin heroine and using a nonsense lyric punctuated by a sharp instrumental riff. Haley's record was slower and funkier. Compare his hip delivery to his corny crooning, it's hard to believe it's the same man. 'Sway With Me' had everyone singing in unison over a cool instrumental track, having the mood of the Diamonds' hit but being sufficiently different to it, unlike the exciting 'The Walkin' Beat' which was so close to 'At The Hop' that Gabler's decision not to release it was doubtless out of fears of litigation.

They must have really enjoyed themselves with the couplets in 'Skinny Minnie', e.g. 'Slightly slimmer than a fishin' pole/She's one half rock, the other half roll', with some to spare which they used the following day for 'Lean Jean'. The other song of this session was written by one Carl Sigman, 'Don't Nobody Move', an exploitation of a new dance fad, the Freeze. Later in the month, Haley was on a week's tour of Florida with the Everly Brothers and Buddy Holly, but closing the show's first half instead of headlining it. Jerry Lee Lewis would not take second billing to anyone; neither did he have to, for at this juncture nobody but Presley was hotter than he. 'Skinny Minnie' (30530) came out at the same time, but surprisingly *Billboard* (March 3) tipped the flip, 'Sway With Me' as the side with hit potential. Many weeks passed before the record appeared in the Top 100: perhaps because 'Sway With Me' was the side getting the action before attention switched to the flip. Even so, just before Haley was about to take off for a month's tour in South America he received the news that 'Skinny Minnie' was breaking nationally. Not much is known about the Latin tour, but Ferguson deemed it important enough to issue a press release to the trade weeklies that whilst there he would be 'visiting art galleries with a view to purchasing masterpieces for the art gallery he co-owned with Haley'. What relevance this had is unclear, but it was relevant to the salaried Comets, for when they got back home they learned that the money that should have been set aside for their pay had been spent on Ferguson's art purchases!

'Skinny Minnie' turned out to be the big hit – if not the smash – Haley badly needed. April 14, it had leapt into the *Billboard*'s Top 100 at 67, going to 43 the following week. By the time the act had returned to the US, Haley had one of the biggest sellers in the country, at No. 32 (May 12), yet he couldn't even pay his own band. Bassist Al Rex was furious and it was probably at this point that he decided he would quit sooner rather than later. Meantime the third album, 'Rockin' Around The World' (8821) was released. What seemed a pointless exercise was no such thing at all and paid for itself several times over in Italy alone. There, 'Piccadilly Rock' was issued as the follow-up to 'Razzle Dazzle' and went to No. 5; next, 'Me Rock A Hula' made No. 4, and by year's end, 'Come Rock With Me', an adaptation of 'O Solo Mio' had also reached No. 4. This gave Haley the impetus for another concept album, getting his cue from the current hit, an LP themed on girls' names ('Bill Haley's Chicks', Decca 8821). It was recorded over four sessions in June, the first on the 3rd, producing 'Chiquita Linda' and a tune not on the album, the bouncy pop instrumental 'Joey's Song', written by Joe Reisman and Sam Gallop, doubtless recorded with Italy in mind, yet curiously it didn't click there. Despite the inevitable low points, e.g. 'Charmaine', the album had its good moments, the belting 'Whoa, Mabel!' and Billy Williamson's vocal, 'B.B. Betty', both written by Haley, Gabler, Keefer and Williamson, whose songs made up about half of its content. Along with 'Corrine, Corrina' and the inclusion of 'Skinny Minnie' and 'Lean Jean', the album had sales potential. These would be Al Rex's final sessions, his place being taken by Al Pompilii, Rudy's cousin. This was the first personnel change in almost three years of the second classic Comets line-up. July, *Billboard* reported that Jolly Joyce was booking new act Al Rex and His Meteors (!). The issue of the 7th reviewed Haley's latest, Decca 30681, tipping 'Don't Nobody Move' as the side with hit potential, presumably because of the fast breaking Tom & Joe hit, 'The Freeze'. 'Skinny Minnie; meanwhile remained strong on the Top 100, it lasting 15 weeks on the chart. Despite *Billboard*'s faith in 'Don't Nobody Move', it was the flip, 'Lean Jean' which took off, it reaching No. 54 on the *Cash Box* national sales chart on August 2. Notwithstanding his revived chart fortunes, Haley was still compelled to take second billing to Jerry Lee Lewis: in a report of a $23,000 grossing show on August 23 in Charlotte (North Carolina), he closed the first half on a bill that included LaVern Baker, The Gladiolas and Bobby Freeman. But on Alan Freed's ten-day 'Big Beat Show' at Brooklyn's Fox Theatre, Haley topped the bill for the first five days in a mouth-watering line-up which included Chuck Berry, Larry Williams, Jack Scott, The Danleers and The Elegants. The Everly Brothers topped the next five days.

Gabler's view that the Haley crew were lacking quality of material was correct, but he was not himself totally blameless. His biggest gaff was turning down 'Weekend', a superb rockin' instrumental written by Pompilii, Beecher and Williamson, cut by the group at Haley's Chester studio. But the boys believed in the record, so went 'undercover' in search of another label to put it out. As the number's publisher, Haley almost certainly approved of this manoeuvre despite the risk. So the record came out on East-West (115), an Atlantic subsidiary – perhaps on account of a previous connection Haley had with the label – with the wonderful 'You Better Believe It' on the flip. Being under contract to Decca, the record could not be pressed under the Comets' name, so an obvious sobriquet was chosen, The Kingsmen ('the king's men). The record took off and made it to 56 in *Cash Box* on September 20. Atlantic now found themselves under pressure to make a group available for personal appearances, so a bogus 'Kingsmen' were created. An EP issued on London-American – Atlantic's British licensees – showed two guitarists, two saxophonists and drummer on the cover. Its tracks were 'Weekend', 'You Better Believe It', and two more by the Comets, 'The Cat Walk' and 'Conga Rock'. We don't know what happened when Decca found out – it is hard to believe that Gabler was unaware of the ruse – but it is significant that just as 'Weekend' was rising on the charts the label chose to make Haley's latest top side an instrumental, 'Chiquita Linda' (30741). In the style of The Champs, it was a strong offering, and coupled with the rousing 'Whoa, Mabel!' there was double-sided hit potential here, yet inexplicably and very disappointingly – considering Haley had seemed to be on the hit trail again – the single made no national impact.

The Comets would moonlight again the following year, as The Lifeguards with 'Everybody Out Of The Pool' on Casa Blanca (5335), the master being picked up by ABC-Paramount (10021) when it looked like becoming a national hit. Earlier (May 1958), Decca put out a record that sounded more like the Comets than they did, The Tyrones' 'Blast Off' (30643) – which fully lived up to its title! What is of interest is that the flip 'I'm Shook', was published by Valley Brook Publishing – so the man did himself have some connection with this most Haley-sounding of releases; likewise the combo's other Decca record (30559), 'Broke Down, Baby', the song also published by Haley's company (February 1958).

We may wonder, after 'Weekend', what other potentially good material Gabler turned down. For example, a tape has come to light of a song Haley submitted for his consideration, 'Football Rock'n'Roll'. The tape is revealing on a number of counts. Haley sings it to his guitar accompaniment with a second voice in support. He explains in detail how it should be presented and arranged and why, if promoted correctly, it could be a hit. He speaks in his usual friendly and affable way and it is clear that this is a man of humour and imagination. It is also clear from this tape that the singer was closely involved in the arrangements and production of all his recordings, Milt Gabler being the man to give them concrete form. The listener can easily imagine the song as a full-blown Haley and the Comets record, certainly better than some of the stuff being put out at the time, yet no more is heard of it.

September, Haley was on a tour of the Canadian provinces of Brunswick and Nova Scotia and in October began a two-month tour of Europe, taking in Switzerland, Belgium and Greece, but significantly not the UK, despite negotiations. Opening at the Paris Olympia, Haley attracted the controversy which he had hoped had become a thing of the past. Kids vandalised seats and poured into the streets chanting, 'Viva Haley!' Worse was to follow in Germany. The scenes at the West Berlin Sportspalast (October 26) were appalling. Rival gangs of leather-clad youths came with missiles and guns loaded with blanks. Storming the stage, they fought with one another, overturning a grand piano, wrecking amplifiers and smashing spotlights. AFN Radio which was there to tape the show had its equipment destroyed. Police could only clear the building by turning on fire hoses. The violence and damage to property continued on the streets and it took the authorities two hours to restore order. Hamburg (27th), Haley fled when kids stormed the stage, leading to a riot which the police quashed with tear gas. At Essen, Haley stopped the show when yobs began throwing missiles at the band. 580 police were on hand to deal with an audience of 6000. Outside, mounted police, dogs and fire hoses were marshalled to break up the mob. The final German date at Stuttgart came as a complete relief: 6000 fans were actually there to enjoy Haley and rock'n'roll and for once he and the boys were able to do a complete set without fear of their lives. It was in Germany Haley re-kindled his acquaintance with Elvis Presley – stationed there as an army private – who joined him backstage at Frankfurt and Stuttgart. What one would have given to be there! Those around Haley must have been relieved, for in the last year or two he had become increasingly touchy about the subject of Presley, to the point where no-one dared mention his name. Another bright spot was working with international singing star Caterina Valente. Both were appearing in the film 'Hier Hin Ich, Hier Bliebe Ich' (Here I Am, Here I Stay), he performing two songs 'Hot Dog, Buddy, Buddy' and a duet with Valenta, 'Viva La Rock'n'Roll'.

December 18, they were back home, just in time for Haley's Christmas shopping and the big party at 'Melody Manor' that was always the highlight of his year. His current single, a solid version of Joe Turner's hit, 'Corrine, Corrine' (flip: 'B.B. Betty, 30783) received a 'Very strong sales potential' rating in *Billboard*, but it did not make the Top 100. January 7, 1959, he was in the Pythian for an inspired session, three numbers he had co-written, but only one, 'The Catwalk' – previously cut by 'The Kingsmen' – an excellent R&R instrumental, would see release. The other two, 'Oragon Rock', Haley's only vocal on this session, was a clever rockin' piece with an oriental theme, and 'ABC Rock', featuring Billy Williamson on vocal as the hip teacher and Frannie Beecher as the kiddie girl pupil. He is hilarious. What a scream: this supremely gifted guitarist, responsible for some of the hottest and cleverest licks in the world of rock'n'roll, could also project the funniest little girl voice! January 29 saw four numbers laid down. Haley again attempted something he should have stayed well clear of, '(Now And Then) There's A Fool Such As I', the second was the catchy, but not earth-shattering 'Be By Me' (composer 'Field'), and the third, the definitely very hip 'Where Did You Go Last Night?" (composer 'Hudgins'), Haley's best performance of the new year. Vocally he's in perfect form, doing the kind of material his voice was tailor made for, and the boys are right on the money with three separate solos, guitar, piano and sax. And how about the lyric: 'I sent you out for a pack of smokes/a pizza pie and a couple of cokes/I ain't bugged about you splittin' the scene/It don't take all night to work a vending machine.' By contrast, Haley adopted a vocal manner that surprised all and sundry with his treatment of 'I Got A Woman'. No-one would guess this was Bill Haley until he hits the high notes, he affecting a decidedly 'black' approach. But really what was wanted was more in the vein of 'Where Did You Go Last Night?'

Unbelievably, the top side of the next single, out mid-February, was 'Charmaine' – from the new LP, 'Bill Haley's Chicks' – a recording described by John Swenson as 'unworthy of a third rate lounge act'. The flip was 'I Got A Woman' (30844). At this point we may think Haley had a death wish and the record deservedly went nowhere. The following single, '(Now And Then There's) A Fool Such As I' was also suicidal, for Presley's version had just crashed the charts and nobody would want to listen to Haley's after hearing his. And we may wonder why 'Where Did You Go Last Night?' was relegated to the flip (30873). April 27, he recorded the two sides of his next single, 'Caledonia' and 'Shaky', both flawless. Whilst 'Shaky' was an in-house composition, 'Caledonia' was, of course, not. What is odd is, that given his preoccupation with controlling publishing, he continued to extensively record outsiders' old material, yet rejecting superior outside tunes written with him in mind. It didn't make sense. Starting in Milwaukee on April 3, Haley swung through a three-week tour of the mid-West with Marty Robbins. The next reported gig was at the Buck Lake Ranch in Angola, Indiana on June 7, two weeks before the release of 'Caledonia' (30926), which despite an appearance on 'The Dick Clark Show' (August 1) also failed to chart nationally. It seemed that whether he delivered dross or solid R&R, the kids weren't listening. It was back to squaresville in August with the issue of 'Ooh! Look-A There, Ain't She Pretty?' (30956), which was recorded on June 19 along with the equally bad '(Thanks For The) Summer Souvenirs' which was never released. It defies belief that Haley thought he could sell this jazz tune: compared to his previous single, 'Caledonia', it seemed the man was a schizophrenic. But then came a surprise: the flip, the bouncy, infectious 'Joey's Song' began to take off. In what seemed a precipitous move, no sooner had it entered *Cash Box*'s Top 100 and already the Comets were cutting an album (September 17 and 24) of instrumentals, which, like 'Joey's Song' was aimed at the Lawrence Welk/Billy Vaughn market. Released in November as 'Strictly Instrumental', it was the fourth and final Decca LP and yet again with no cover picture of the act. Why was this? The album was bassist Al Rappa's first, Al Pompilii having left after a year's service.

The single turned into a sizeable hit, climbing to No. 35 during November and staying on the chart into the new year. The equally commercial and very Billy Vaughn-ish 'Skokiaan (South African Song)' (31030, flip: 'Puerto Rican Peddlar'), from the LP, which was also selling well, entered *Billboard*'s 'Hot 100' on January 10, 1960, and would rise to No. 70 (83 in *Cash Box*). This and the next release, '(Put Another Nickel In) Music! Music! Music!'/'Strictly Instrumental' (31080), would be Bill Haley and His Comets 26th and 27th final singles, for their contract had expired in September, which may explain the rush to record the LP. With the act hot again, the label was keen to renew the contract. But Haley had a problem. He was deep in debt and the bulk of his record royalties were being seized by the Internal Revenue Service, which had served papers on Decca. Haley didn't even see the money – it went straight from the label to the taxman. It would seem he didn't want to leave Decca – why should he, for he had the best producer and one of the biggest, and most honest, companies – but he needed a big advance on a renewed contract in order to be left with something for himself and the boys. The label couldn't justify a big advance, for Haley was not the big star he once was, so he had another idea. If he signed with another label and received a substantial advance, the IRS would not know and he would get to keep all the money. Well, *all* the money, probably not. As if being in debt to the IRS was not bad enough, he had an even more sinister creditor. Teetering on bankruptcy, he could not even pay his hotel bills and travelling expenses, Jim Ferguson turned to the Mob for financial assistance who obliged. What was received and on what terms we don't know, but needless to say Haley was heading for deeper trouble, not less. But, for a moment, the sun shone again. Warner Brothers accepted him with open arms, advancing $50,000 and his first sessions were already booked for January. So he entered the new decade on a high note, not only was he on the domestic charts, 'Joey's Song' had gone to No. 1 in Australia; he had a lucrative new recording contract, and to top it all, Cuppy was soon to give birth to their fourth son, Scott.

7. Change

The debut single on the new label was a complete surprise and raised a few questions. Neither side had anything to do with rock'n'roll. The top side, 'Candy Kisses' (WB5145), revisited a song Haley had first done in '48, hillbilly-come-pop balladry in new clothes; whilst the flip, 'Tamiami', another bright instrumental novelty, also had little to offer the kids, yet this was the side to take off, entering the *Cash Box* Top 100 on February 20 and reaching 79. What this single tells us is that, whilst Haley was on a new label, it did not signify a new start. Haley was only on the new label, after all, for the hefty cash advance. Warner producer George Avakian was not moulding or reshaping him, any more than Milt Gabler could, for musically Haley was always his own man. Early 1960 in the US was a bleak place for a Fifties rocker. 1959 had seen a dramatic and decisive shift in teenagers' tastes from R&R to emasculated pubescent pop. A new crop of teenage idols had appeared, pretty boys average age 19. Record companies saw the future in these, or at least the future in terms of the next two years. The R&R frontliners of 1955-58 were consigned to limbo, only Presley both surviving and flourishing and that because he was selling sex. If he hadn't that and only R&R, he would have found himself in exactly the same position as Haley. In any event, Presley had ditched R&R, he didn't need it and the fickle American public didn't miss it. Haley had only managed to get into the new decade's charts with happy instrumental ditties. He knew the writing was on the wall for him and he had to think outside R&R. A teenage idol he could not be, so the only other viable option was to restyle himself as a crooner. Which is the only explanation we can find for 'Candy Kisses'. But there is one crucial difference between this and his latter day limp crooning on Decca, vocally he had managed to minimise his natural sentimentality, projecting himself instead in a more believable manner. This, and the subsequent Warner recordings, were to bring something unexpected: Haley, hitherto an embarrassingly sentimental singer, who should have stayed instead with R&R, was now proving that he *could* be a convincing crooner. Certainly his phrasing and delivery is stronger and more confident: something had definitely changed between Decca and Warner and the answer may have lain with Avakian. All the Warner sessions were done at the Bell studio in New York, a favoured location by both major and minor labels alike, the sound being somehow lighter and cleaner. There is a remarkable technical perfection and indeed Haley and the Comets would never sound more musical. An album was recorded, simply entitled 'Bill Haley & His Comets', consisting entirely of his versions of Fifties' hits. This, on the other hand, seemed like a retrograde step, reinforcing his connection with the past rather than the future. It was roughly split between ballads ('I Almost Lost My Mind', 'Love Letters In The Sand', 'My Special Angel', etc.) and rockers, including three remakes of his own hits, 'Rock Around The Clock', given the same rhythmic bounce as the '57 'Rock The Joint', and 'Crazy, Man, Crazy', which both worked well. Less impressive is 'Shake, Rattle And Roll' and its loose, almost Ray Charles-type treatment – but it does have one unintentionally amusing moment. Haley struggles to keep a straight face after the line, 'I'm like a one-eyed cat ...' which in his case was literally true, and we may assume someone in the studio was poking fun at him at this particular moment. We usually hear that Haley was very touchy about any reference to his bad eye, but this unexpected unguarded moment gives us a different glimpse of the man. Noteworthy is that of the others' hits he performs there is only one of whom he performs twice: Fats Domino. I would suggest that if there was one act from the era that Haley most admired it was Domino. Aware of his own limitations, it must have impressed and encouraged him that Domino, 'old' and devoid of sex appeal, could command such popularity, enjoying hits before him and after him, and often with R&R treatments of standards. Haley's constant flirtation with standards was, I believe, a bid to capitalise on Domino's market, but the problem was he could never get it right whilst Domino had an unerring ear for the right song and the right arrangement – and then he had *that* voice. The LP's highlight, however, is 'Whole Lotta Shakin' Goin' On', a powerful, raunchy workout of the Lewis classic, which again underlines Haley's mastery of the idiom he was born for.

In April, his second single, 'Chick Safari'/'Hawk' (5154) came out, at the same time as his last Decca single, 'Skokian' – a tune Rudy Pompilii would have been well familiar with, for it was a smash for Ralph Marterie in '54. 'Chick Safari', a Haley-Keefer-Cafra tune (note the lyric, 'Deep in the blackboard jungle'), was a fine side, demonstrating that both Haley and Warner were now serious about a new direction. It was the closest thing to a Haley solo record, for the singer's strong presence, augmented by Warner's session singers, dominated. The record had an infectious haunting quality, which was well received by the trade weeklies along with the flip side, a finger-snapping 'Fever'-type production. Both sides reveal a Bill Haley never heard before: born to rock he was, but here was proof positive that he was not a one-trick pony. But here's an odd twist: just as Warner was pushing the new sounding Haley, what must he have thought when he heard a record – rising on the charts at that very moment – by one Sammy Masters called 'Rockin' Red Wing'. Here it is spring 1960 and amidst all the sweet teen fodder there comes blasting over the airwaves a record that is pure 1957 Haley, except that it *isn't* Bill! One's immediate thought on hearing it is that the Comets are moonlighting again and that both the song and Masters are fronts for something that Warner didn't want Haley to record: but no such thing.

Such an anomaly was typical of the period. The record industry itself was profoundly conservative and unimaginative – many decades later it still is – and as teenage slosh was in the ascendant that was what it backed. But the Top 100 was open to allcomers and anything daring and innovative almost always came not from the majors but from tiny maverick labels. Most of the unexpected hits of the next two years came left field from this quarter. The likes of 'Angel Baby' (Rosie & The Originals), 'Quarter To Three'(U.S. Bonds) and 'Monster Mash' (Bobby 'Boris' Pickett) would never have been touched by the majors in a thousand years, for they did not understand them. The record industry was never run by R&R fans, for if it were and if Warner, for example, believed in the music it would have encouraged Haley to 'go back' instead of 'forward'. This would not have been bad business: indeed the path Warner did take with Haley turned out to be bad business. As elsewhere in life, 'progress' does not always mean progress.

Whilst Sammy Masters was hitting in the States with the Haley sound, the man himself was clicking in a new market: Mexico. April, he was there for appearances in night clubs; also TV and film work. Little could he know at the time how significant this new territory would become. But all was not well, for the first 'Comets revolt' since '55 was brewing. Speculation is that Haley may not have got paid on some Mexican gigs and he – a man with no financial reserve – could not pay them. But it may have gone deeper than that, for not getting paid had become a regular hazard of the salaried Comet. The final session featuring drummer Ralph Jones was on June 1 for the third single, 'So Right Tonight' and 'Let The Good Times Roll, Creole' (5171). It had been only a matter of time before Haley got lumbered with the 'cute girlie' chorus, so beloved of record producers of the time, but 'So Right Tonight' still comes out sounding good. A Haley-Keefer-Bob Hayes composition, rhythmically it bears a resemblance to Presley's 'I Need Your Love Tonight', but by far the better side was the flip which really belts. Following this single, Pompilii and Beecher quit, Rudy's departure coming as a big surprise as 'loyalty' was his middle name. He, Beecher and Jones then worked as The Merrymen back in their home territory of Chester, not as exciting as being Comets, maybe, but at least they got paid and got to sleep in their own beds.

Australia remained a good market as 'Tamiami' climbed the charts there in June, but the home market would again ignore his latest single, the trade ads for which showed a rather chubby Haley ('A pizza pie and a couple of cokes'!) He also looked a little chubby on the front cover of both his Warner albums, he wearing the same suit from what was obviously the same photo session. Remarkably, he had recorded the second album within a month of the first. Entitled 'Bill Haley's Juke Box', it was the one and only time Haley had recorded an entire album of ballads, all country hits of the last decade or so, again emphasising his connection with the past, this one even ignoring the audience that had given him his hits. It was as if Haley had come full circle since 1949, and whilst one might have had reservations about the wisdom of this project, it would still have been nice if it had sold. He had been robbed of his bid for country stardom by 'Rock The Joint' and with the fall of R&R he clearly thought the time was right to try again, but the album was not in tune with current country trends. Milt Gabler didn't think he could hack it in the modern country scene and tried to steer him away from it; Warner indulged him and wound up with a dud. Unlike Decca, the label put Haley on the LP covers, but interestingly not the Comets; and indeed the 'Juke Box' is almost presented as a solo project. This was almost certainly Warner's idea and not Haley's, but will not have relieved tensions building in the band. And again one wonders why Haley, who desperately needed publishing revenue more than ever, recorded two albums without one Haley original. The probable explanation is that, as Gabler had observed in the final two years, Haley and the Comets were less and less prepared for new material, it being easier for them to record tunes that were a staple of their stage act and requiring little rehearsal for the studio.

As it turned out, Warner soon lost interest. The label was enjoying smash hit singles by The Everly Brothers ('Cathy's Clown', etc.), Connie Stevens ('16 Reasons') and Bob Luman ('Let's Think About Livin''), as well as monster selling albums by Bob Newhart. By comparison, Haley seemed like small fry, hardly worth spending time on. Almost a year went by before the label had him back in the studio for what would turn out to be his final Warner record, 'Flip, Flop And Fly'/'Honky Tonk'. A year had gone by and Haley still couldn't come up with one single new tune for a new record. The rift with Pompilii and Beecher had been healed, for they reappear on this record; but 'Jonesy' had gone for good. In the States, he had observed that the writing was on the wall for Haley, who could now enter and exit a venue without fear of being even noticed, let alone mobbed, and he didn't fancy spending the rest of his life working for a has-been in foreign dives for little or no money. That was his view, which may not have seemed very charitable, but one suspects still other reasons for Jones' departure which flatter Haley even less; yet Pompilii and Beecher returned, but they always had stronger connections with the boss. Meanwhile the two original partners, Billy Williamson and Johnny Grande, remained committed. Jones' place as drummer was taken by David Bates.

'Flip, Flop And Fly' deservedly went nowhere. The pointless Latin rhythm distracted from the song's impact and the vocal was submerged in the mix. Johnny Bell's remains the definitive R&R version; Haley was out of touch here, unlike the instrumental flip, a rousing revival of Bill Doggett's 'Honky Tonk'. R&R instrumentals – unlike vocals – continued to regularly hit the charts in the early 60s and one wonders if Warner could have done more to get this one off the ground and what were they thinking to relegate it to the flip of the inferior top side? But, as we have seen, it seems as if the label had lost interest anyway.

The single came out about the same time as the second trip to Mexico (May), which included an appearance in his second film there, 'Juventude Rebelde', the title, 'Young Rebels', being instructive, for yet again, no matter what the country or the market, Haley's name is inextricably linked to teenage delinquency. His Mexican films – there were more – involved no acting, his grasp of the language was minimal, he and the Comets merely providing the background in night club scenes, etc. It was probably on this trip that he met Maria Velasao, a beautiful dancer, more of whom later.

Big changes were afoot. Haley and Warner parted company and the end of an era came with the sale of his Chester three-floor office and studio building. It was also probably the end of Haley's own booking agency for promoting other acts. It had been run for him by an experienced booking agent, Jim Feddis, who had both a dim view of Haley's eye for talent and his business methods: 'They spent (money) faster than they made it ... Haley was moody and dumb, and he thought he was smart. When Haley talked to you he was figuring out how he was going to screw you later on' (quoted by kind permission of W.H. Allen & Co. Ltd., publishers of John Swenson's excellent biography, 'Bill Haley'). By Feddis' reference to 'they' we presume he means Ferguson. It's hard to say how corrupted, if at all, were Williamson and Grande by their involvement, but 'If you lay down with dogs, you get fleas'. Even if they were untainted, it is almost certain they were also investigated, if not hounded by the IRS, in its bid to unravel Haley and Ferguson's shambolic scams and tax dodges. Although we are not expressly told, there must have been tensions within the partnership, and all at a time when their fortunes were in decline. Doubtless the sale of the Chester office and studio was made out of dire necessity, but to whom did the proceeds go: the tax man or the Mob? The extent of his debt to the Mob is unknown and the IRS' suspicions may have by this time brought him to the attention of the FBI. In any event, the next two labels he would record for, Gone and Roulette of New York, were both Mob-affiliated. But despite the end of Haley's Chester business activities, his long time confidante Jack Howard would continue to administer his publishing interests.

It is July 25, 1961, and the Haley crew are in the Bell Sound studio recording for Gone. The No. 1 record on the Top 100 is 'Quarter To Three' by the kiss-curled U.S. Bonds – whose previous smash, 'New Orleans' had become a staple of the Comets' act – with Chubby Checker's 'Let's Twist Again' closing in. Cue 'The Spanish Twist' backed by another twister, 'My Kind Of Woman', both Haley's strongest sides in a while and certainly for years to come. To Pompilii's infectious Mexican refrain, Haley describes the joys of the new dance before an exciting drumming spot punctuated by a short sharp twist sax solo and closing with a memorable wordless chorus. It was as good as any of the Twist hits of the day and Haley and the Comets' performance was bang on the money. 'My Kind Of Woman' begins with a Ray Charles-type electric piano from Grande and really drives between rapid chord change bursts, with a torrid sax solo rounding off an exciting track. Haley's performance is perfect. Whilst both sides could not be strictly speaking classified as 'rock'n'roll' they demonstrated the act's power to deliver to a contemporary market. At least, musically speaking, Haley was no 'has been'. 'My Kind Of Woman' was co-written by Mickey Lee Lane, perhaps another local attraction, for he would have a hit, 'Shaggy Dog' in 1964 on the Philadelphian Swan label. Various composers are cited for the top side. Dellabarea-Cruz are the supposed writers for the song, which the lyric suggests, 'began down in Mexico', whilst sight of the Gone (5111) disc shows 'Anne Thompson' as the composer; yet in Britain, where the record was released on London-American, 'The' is deleted from the title, 'Bradford' is shown as the writer! But whomever the writer, royalties would have wound up in only one place – the Mafia. And there *were* royalties, for the disc garnered substantial airplay in both American and British markets, the latter clocking up sales of 50,000 during 1962, a higher figure than many records making the *NME* Top 30 at the time. Yet it did not even make the record trade's *Record Retailer* Top 50, which makes our reliance on chart statistics only as the measurement of popularity unsafe. The problem is that charts are based on speed of sales: if a record sells slowly, like 'Spanish Twist', it won't chart. We rely on charts' data, for they are all we have, and I wish it was otherwise.

In the US, the Gone (5116) follow-up was disappointing: two instrumentals, 'Riviera' – which interestingly shows the composer credit as an Italian not previously encountered – and 'Warpaint', the better side, penned by Billy Williamson. South of the border, Haley's fortunes were waxing. He had been back there a third time in September, signing a record deal with the all-important local Orfeon label – which had better foresight than the American majors who now wouldn't touch Haley with a barge pole. He immediately cut an album, 'Twist', the first of a remarkable eight LPs. One track was 'Florida Twist', written by a Chester record dealer, Anthony Caruso, yet Pompilii's name appeared on the disc's label as a co-writer. Pompilii cut himself on 50% of Caruso's tune as his price for recording it. We have already seen how Haley & co. liked to muscle in on others' composing rights and it is dispiriting to see the likeable and honest Pompilii indulging in this immoral practice (but commonplace in those days and usually associated with unscrupulous minor record labels). 'Florida Twist', an instrumental, so ridiculously basic that it beggars belief that it needed two people to write it, so transparent is the scam, became a Mexican smash. Pompilii was handsomely rewarded for his tactic, but Caruso could hardly complain, for little could he imagine that something so trite could be so successful.

Bill Haley had hit paydirt again. 'Florida Twist' went to No. 1 in Mexico and within a few months became the country's biggest selling act, charting four singles simultaneously, duplicating the fabulous success he had enjoyed years earlier, but this time as the 'King of Twist', not R&R. Whilst the rest of the world thought the Twist king was Chubby Checker, no-one could imagine that in Mexico it was the forgotten Bill Haley. Whilst the debut album was yet at No. 1 on the Mexican

LP charts, the second 'Bikini Twist' was already out and selling fast. The Orfeon albums were contemporary dance fodder, often badly recorded, consisting of simple riffs cooked up by the group, versions of current and recent US hits, and Haley's Spanish rendering of 'Let's Twist Again' and the like, plus the inevitable and forgettable Spanish versions of the Decca hits. Despite reservations about Mexican pay being less than US, not to mention the risks of not getting paid at all, the Comets enjoyed personal appearances, fans regarding Pompilii and Beecher with the same awe as Haley. But despite such admiration, Beecher had to quit again, for the long absences from home was straining his marriage, and this time his departure was for good, his place taken by Johnny Kay. But whilst he and the others were worried about their wives and families, they were aghast at Haley's open cavorting with Martha Velasao. The devoted family man, who would never tolerate any hanky panky in the band, evidently paid no heed to the fact that Cuppy happened also to be a close friend of theirs and their families. Back home, Beecher would spend the rest of his working life as a factory worker in Norristown, but he played one more time for his former boss when Haley offered him $500 for three nights at New York's Round Table Club and a limousine to take him home each night. On an 11-day (March 1962) residency at the club, a live album was to be recorded on the three nights Beecher was present. Round Table owner, the very shady Morris Levy, also owner of Roulette Records, had a bright idea for reviving Haley's American fortunes. Roulette was red hot at the time with a live album cut at the local Peppermint Lounge by Joey Dee & The Starliters. Levy, impressed by Haley's potential with 'The Spanish Twist', and aware of the singer's sudden Twist star status south of the border, believed the Dee formula could work a second time. The album was made up of old tunes and new, all given the Twist treatment, Haley as usual spreading the performance between his own vocals and Williamson's and various instrumentals. It is perhaps only at this time we ever hear Haley singing slow, albeit in dance tempo, when he eases the pace for 'Waltzing The 1-2-3 Twist', which grinds nicely with the sax and a Joe Turner blues, 'I Want A Little Girl', highlighted by a powerful Pompilii solo. As usual, it is The Comets who give the show, but its star is undeniably Franny Beecher whose spots on 'Down By The Riverside Twist' and 'Whistlin' And Walkin' Twist' are nothing short of sensational. Joey Dee's drummer, 'Sticks' Evans was brought in to get the perfect Twist beat, to the annoyance of the group, for it meant more work when in point of fact Evans was no better than their own. Presumably the label thought the Dee hit magic would rub off on Haley, but the album, 'Twistin' Knights At The Round Table' (Roulette 25174) went nowhere, not even a single being issued from it. In any event, the 11-day stint at the club should have gone a long way to alleviating Haley's debt to the outfit.

The third Orfeon album, 'Twist En Mexico', came out as Haley's popularity was spreading to other Central American states, his Latin appeal further emphasised by the sudden success in Italy of 'Music! Music! Music!', two years after it came out in the States. Yet Haley's private life was in turmoil. He seemed to have taken up permanent residence in Mexico, now hiding not only from the IRS but also his wife. The once happy and affluent 'Melody Manor' had now become a place where 'not even a loaf of bread could be found'. Yet he still made forays into the US – and Canada – lured by cash-in-hand gigs, and there is reference to Haley in Chester reduced to sleeping on Pompilii's couch, shunned at 'Melody Manor' and no money for even a cheap hotel, John Swenson describing him as 'leaving a trail of debts and enemies'. One is baffled by such impoverishment at a time of such success. It seems at this time, Haley's drinking got worse. Back in '57, he locked himself in his hotel room, pining for home and family and drinking gallons of coffee. A month later in England, Cuppy noticed him drinking more liquor than he should. We may assume that between '57 and '62 the boozing intensified. On the other hand, he must have been sober whilst around his senorita and her family. Perhaps he was drunk north of the border and sober south of it. Aptly for a heavy drinker, he was also a heavy smoker and probably always was: we may recall that as a lad it was he who introduced his pals to the weed.

Losing 'Melody Manor' in the divorce settlement shattered Haley and we can only imagine his anguish at being separated from his children. Getting at the facts during this dark period is difficult due to the understandable reticence on the part of those around Haley. Johnny Grande was heavily demoralised and had the embarrassment of dealing with hotel management about damage to rooms, so much for 'Bill, the nice guy'. Meanwhile, the act worked continuously and not just in the Americas. September 1962 saw the boys in a two-week residency at Hamburg's Star-Club, where the support acts were British beat groups that would soon become household names, before a tour of US army bases. Then Grande quit, his health and his marriage not in a good state. Arriving home, he slung his accordion from the porch, desperately disillusioned, his decade-long partnership with Haley not worth a pile of beans. It was probably in November that Haley was in Las Vegas recording an album for a label called Guest Star. It was seemingly a cash-in-hand deal; no contract, no receipts: for apart from evading tax, he was apparently already signed to another label, presumably Newtown Records of Philadelphia. Apart from two mediocre re-cuts of 'See You Later, Alligator' and 'ABC Boogie', it consisted of indifferent contemporary material by unknown writers, including 'Altar Of Love', noteworthy for the Fats Domino-type delivery. Haley handled all vocals on the set. It came out probably January 1963 on Guest Star 1954 entitled 'Bill Haley, Rock-A-Round The Clock King'. At least, unlike the Roulette LP, it sported a picture of Haley, in a blue tuxedo and in an animated pose, without guitar, he looking slimmer and tanned, but noticeably older. The two re-cuts were issued as a single on Kacy (7005). In a separate development, it was probably in February that an instrumental, 'Yakety Sax', was issued on Logo (also No. 7005) to cash in on Boots Randolph's breaking national hit of the same name. The owners of these shadowy enterprises had the temerity to put the name of Boots Randolph on the label, when in fact it was Rudy Pompilii and the Comets. The flip, 'Boots' Blues' was genuinely by Randolph, for Guest Star had acquired several of his early masters. Meanwhile, south of the border, the fourth Orfeon LP was released, 'Madison', which showcased Pompilii's treatment of big band tunes.

It was about this time – perhaps January and certainly not long after Grande's exit – that Billy Williamson departed, the last of the original Saddlemen and partners. The steel guitarist whose 'lightning flashes' gave the edge to Haley's classics, ideas man and comic, the most frequent alternative vocalist, was gone. And he was gone for good.

Never again would be speak to anyone about his time with Haley. He died of cancer in 1986. His place was taken by Nick Nastos, only he and Johnny Kay (lead guitar) and Al Rappa (bass) retaining any kind of status amongst fans. Rudy Pompilii was the last remaining 'classic' Comet whom, in the fulness of time, of course, would serve longer than any other. He was now, in effect, the Comets' boss, hiring, firing, rehearsing and paying the men. Promoters and agents would pay Haley direct – for Ferguson was already out of it, Jolly Joyce managing at one point for an unknown duration – and he kept the lion's share of the fee: Pompilii took the next biggest cut and distributed what was left to the others, according to their status and longevity. Junior members would feel hard done by and there was a regular turnover of Comets. Moreover, there were arrangements for temporaries picked up when and wherever, in the end the act becoming little better than a touring pick-up band.

Haley married Maria Velasao and began his third family and he converted to her Roman Catholic faith, although not straight away apparently. They lived on a ranch, presumably at Juarez, just across the border from El Paso. How the ranch was financed and also the various non-musical business enterprises that he now ventured upon is unknown, though the obvious explanation is income from his successful Mexican career; but this is the same man whom at other times could not afford a hotel room or buy a car (apparently the illicit Guest Star transaction was a desperate bid to raise cash for an auto he needed immediately). He was a disaster in business, and worse still, he learned nothing from his mistakes and the new ventures also ended in grief.

Four singles were put out by Newtown, all in '63, none of which were memorable or distinguished. Newtown had hit paydirt earlier with Patti LaBelle & The Blue Belles whose records possessed an unpolished quality which typified the label and also Haley's releases. The label seemed an odd choice for the singer, though perhaps he was in no position to choose, for it aimed at the R&B and pop market with the typical teen-gimmick fodder of the day, but to which Haley adapted very well. It is interesting that during this time he operated within the contemporary R&B field. Had he pursued his career more sensibly and soberly (literally!), he could have remained on major labels in the Sixties, receiving strong material and scoring with numbers readily associated with acts like Chubby Checker, The Dovells and Freddie Cannon; but instead he was stuck with inferior material and unimaginative productions. Newtown should be glad that the first single, 'Tenor Man' (5013) wasn't a hit, for if it had been, it would have been stung by a lawsuit from the publishers of the Fats Domino hit, 'What A Party' which it plainly plagiarised. The flip was 'Up Goes My Love'. The following single, 'Midnight In Washington' (5014), an instrumental, which despite its clever play on the title of Kenny Ball's hit, had no connection. The flip was 'White Parakeets', the single being issued under the curious name of 'B.H. Sees Combo'. 5024, 'Dance Around The Clock', was a song Haley clearly believed in for he featured it regularly on stage, perhaps in some forlorn hope that the 'clock' idea could work again, and it would work again, but not with this song! The flip, 'What Can I Say After I Said I Was Sorry?', suggests a nice country ballad, but it is nothing of the sort and hard to remember half an hour after hearing it. 5025 was 'Tandy'/'You Call Everybody Darling', and there was an earlier release, 5011, not by Haley but featuring the Comets backing Carrie Grant & The Grandeurs on 'Mish-Mash' and 'Let The Girls Sing'.

The Newtown sides were deservedly flops, with the exception of 'Tenor Man' which saw release in Britain and – as always here – enjoyed good sales. The next label on which Haley would appear would be ... Decca! For a man who bore the lion's share of his own recent misfortunes, Haley was extraordinarily lucky. Outside of Mexico, he was a 'has been'. Mexico itself was an astonishing piece of good luck, rejuvenating not only his career but also his private life. Crushed by the separation from his family and loss of his beautiful home, he was to experience all over again the joys of a new wife, home and family. This man's life was full of the unexpected and the paradoxical. The international scene was being revolutionised by the beat group explosion from England, bringing with it a still newer generation of young fans. Haley was now removed two 'generations' from the one in which he enjoyed his greatest success, the middle one, 1959-64, the teen idol and dance craze era with its 13-18 year old fans, giving way to the newest crop obsessed with the Beatles and co. Early 1964, Haley seemed even more remote; most thirteen- and fourteen-year-olds had no idea who he was and couldn't care less. This was a completely different world from the present where musically there is virtually no change. Today, acts can indulge five or ten years in preparing an album and find their fans coming out in droves when it's eventually released. Back then, that was unthinkable: delay a new album by five years, an act would find both fans and market vanished. The styles of 1964 were far removed from 1959, but you can hardly tell the difference between 2009 and 1989. Given this picture, Haley should have been well and truly consigned to history. So what happens? Thousands of miles away from Mexico and Europe, 'Rock Around The Clock' enters the Australian charts! What brought this about is unknown, but it brought with it another unexpected development. Decca was earning yet again from its former star, so Haley figured that this was an opportune moment to phone Milt Gabler to see if he would take him back. We may be surprised at Gabler's response, considering the following. We will recall that he was the co-writer of a lot of Haley's material, owned by the singer's publishing company, and that his idea of 'Skinny Minnie' gave Haley a boost when he badly needed it. *But Gabler never received a single cent in royalties from Haley's publishing firm.*

In other words, Gabler, whom had been extremely lucky for Haley – perhaps the single most important individual in his career – had been conned by the singer.

Someone else would have told Haley to take a hike, but not Gabler. In photographs and in snippets of conversation heard on session tapes, Gabler comes across as grumpy, yet his nature was quite different. He had always seemed to have a soft spot for Haley – the singer's paradox was that it was hard to dislike him, yet he made enemies – and was inclined to blame Jim Ferguson for his misfortunes (though in reality, both manager and artist were of dubious character). Gabler argued Haley's case to the Decca hierarchy, urging a contract for the singer, 'The poor guy's down and out. He made a lot of money for us and he could make it again. Who could have guessed at the Mexican thing and it might just happen for him again here.' Management wasn't impressed, but with the news from Festival – Decca's Australian licensee – that 'Rock Around The Clock' was heading towards the Top Three, a compromise was suggested: Haley would be given one shot with one single. If it did well, then a contract would be considered. So on June 16, Haley and the Comets were in the Pythian Temple to record 'The Green Door' – the old Jim Lowe hit – and 'Yeah, She's Evil'. Johnny Kay was on lead guitar with Abie Baker on bass (presumably, Rappa was indisposed, for he had not left the group); Dave Martin played piano and Dave Holly drummed. The result was unquestionably the best record since 'Spanish Twist'. Gabler's magic is all over it with steel guitar evident and classic riffing from Pompilii, all coming together in an exciting crescendo mid-way. Haley is in top form with a colourful and lively delivery. There was just one thing wrong: it was the wrong song. Even in '64 when I learnt that this was Haley's choice I was dismayed. This song just didn't belong in the teenage world of 1964. Haley gets this golden opportunity to get back with his old label and blows it by picking a song like this: was he so bereft of imagination? At the same time, Little Richard and Chuck Berry were hitting the charts with songs redolent of their former glory, yet Haley couldn't hack it. Curiously enough, such are the uncertainties of public taste, that years later Shakin' Stevens would get a smash out of 'Green Door' – in itself far from being a bad song – thanks to Stuart Colman's dynamic production, which was right on the money at the time. The flip of Decca 31650 demonstrated Haley and The Comets' mastery of the R&B-soul idiom and made a good coupling.

8. Revival

But Haley's fortunes were again on the up and up. Immediately before the Decca session, he played to no less than 30,000 at a Berlin venue. He must have found this immensely reassuring, given that in the States the best that he could get was small clubs with invariably indifferent audiences. Then, in July, an early recording by the Beatles backing Tony Sheridan singing 'Skinny Minnie' entered the German Top Fifty. It became a big hit, reaching No. 3 and spending a remarkable 28 weeks on chart. Buckets of songwriting and publishing income for Haley. Moreover, there is also income from a version by Gerry & The Pacemakers, one of the biggest groups at the time. Jack Howard, who had continued to administer Haley's publishing interests, then had the gall to ask Milt Gabler if he would sell his stake in 'Skinny Minnie'. The producer reminded Howard that he had never seen a cent from the song in the first place. We don't know at what point this took place: I would hazard a guess that it was about the time of the 'Green Door' session or very soon after. Haley and Howard would have got wind of 'Skinny Minnie' breaking in Germany and knew that with the Beatles' touch it could be a big one. Gabler may not have been aware of this yet, so if Howard bought his share now that would avoid obligation over future royalty payments. We may marvel at Gabler's relaxed approach – he felt pity for Haley, a man who endured personal tragedy whilst at the peak of stardom and who would lose that also – for he agreed to sell. He received a derisory $38.

The cheque bounced.

Milt Gabler, the man who gave Haley a second chance, who believed in his talent and pitied his circumstances, was conned again.

One also wonders at how much Grande, and in particular Williamson, received for their composing credits. Both had quit very unhappy and disillusioned men and Williamson's lasting silence spoke for itself.

July 1964, Tony Sheridan is climbing in Germany. 'Rock Around The Clock' is Top Ten in Australia: and now, in the States, 'Clock' is breaking in mid-West markets. Remarkable.

In the UK, the Warner version of 'Clock' had been issued. Why there was this sudden international interest in the song is unknown, but despite a major plug on the TV show, 'Thank Your Lucky Stars' when it was made its 'Record Of The Week', it failed to chart. But Haley was about to stray back into British consciousness when in September he arrived for his first tour since the big one of '57. Previous attempts to return Haley to the UK in 1958 and 1962 had failed, but promoter Don Arden proved third time lucky when he organised the 'King and Queen of Rock'n'Roll' tour with Brenda Lee. He and the Comets – which, with Pompilii and Rappa, consisted of Johnny Kay, Nick Nastos and Dave Holly –

appeared on 'Ready, Steady, Go!' performing 'Green Door' – the record released to coincide with the tour – and a thrilling 'Rudy's Rock' and 'Rock Around The Clock'. Haley also appeared as a panelist judging new records on 'Ready, Steady, Win!' The tour proper did not begin until about ten days after Haley's arrival, a punishing 27-day trek with not a single day off. It was a tour of surprises and conundrums, beginning with the dilemma of Brenda Lee's unavailability. In her place was a vastly different act, Manfred Mann, then on a hot winning hit streak and about as far removed from Haley as you could get. Moreover, the supporting acts were also of the beat group genre with little or no connection with rock'n'roll. Haley and the Comets also did several separate gigs, solo and with Gene Vincent; more often they were not only doing two shows nightly with the Mann package but also travelling to another place to substitute for Little Richard whom had (characteristically) not shown up. The tour kicked off in Ireland (September 16), travelling to ten towns in five days, before a grand swing through England, Scotland and Wales.

The tour inevitably exposed a clash of youth cultures, the teeny boppers on the one hand clamouring for Manfred Mann and co., and on the other, the mid-twenties' Haley fans, many, if not most, of whom despised the likes of Mann and the contemporary music scene. Whilst the older fans were unhappy that Haley had secondary billing closing the first half – this was not unreasonable for Haley hadn't had a Top 20 hit in seven years, whilst the Mann group were currently enjoying hit after hit – they at least had the choice of not enduring the final half. The pubescents who screamed their lungs out for Mann were dumb and bewildered during Haley's spot, which told us more about them than Haley. The singer's act was the same as it always had been, with the Comets doing most of the work whilst he handled vocals on five or six numbers, usually 'Razzle Dazzle', 'Shake, Rattle And Roll', 'See You Later, Alligator', 'Saints Rock'n'Roll' and 'Rock Around The Clock'. At solo gigs, he might add 'Rock-A-Beatin' Boogie' and 'Rock The Joint'. The other vocals were by Pompilii, Rappa and Kay, performing variously hits by Chuck Berry, Little Richard, Tommy Tucker and US Bonds. Nick Nastos would provide a highlight with a virtuoso rendering of 'Malaquera', which usually went down well, Haley allowing him an encore on one or two more Spanish-themed tunes. But there was a slickness and almost soul-less quality to the act. By this time, British rock'n'roll fans had been thrilled by the dynamite performances of the likes of Gene Vincent and Jerry Lee Lewis, and in particular Little Richard, which made Haley's act seem formularistic and without 'edge'; there being a sense that perhaps his attitude was 'Let's get this set done and get the hell out of here'. There was never a sense of this at a show by Vincent, Lewis or Richard: they had 'edge' in bucketfuls and mesmerised by their presence. Haley did not mesmerise. Hugh McCallum, Haley's British fan club secretary, whom the singer appointed as his Press Secretary for the tour, urged him to sing more songs, but he would not budge. McCallum idolised Haley, yet had the gumption to address his shortcoming and the courage to confront him with it; but if he couldn't make him change his mind, no-one could. But still early in the tour (25th, Finsbury Park, London) came a surprise: Haley closed the show in both houses, a development which apparently remained unchanged for the rest of the tour, with the chart-topping Manfred Mann relegated to closing the first half. The reason for this change is unclear, but at Kilburn in London (Oct. 5) we hear of 2000 Haley fans packing in the second house and an attempt to storm the stage! This got into the newspapers, bringing a sense of *déjà vu*. By the time the tour ended, Haley was shattered and down with the flu, unable to go to Stockholm to cover another Little Richard no-show.

Back in the US, late 1964 and 1965 saw the release of three singles on the Apt label, also recorded at New York's Bell Studio, the first, presumably a Comets instrumental, 'Big Daddy'/'St Louis Blues' (25051), issued under the name of The Merrymen (Or Merri-Men, according to another source). The other two, 'Burn That Candle'/'Stop, Look And Listen' (25081) and 'Tongue Tied Tony'/ 'Haley A Go Go' (25087) proved neither Apt nor Haley had any idea where they were going. 'Candle' is an inferior contemporary re-make of his hit. Meanwhile, he remained in demand for personal appearances around the world, including American Air Force bases in Germany, Mexico – where he appeared for ten consecutive weeks on the 'Orfeon A Go Go' TV show – Canada, South America, Australia and South Africa. Haley has a young wife and a young family and yet he hardly sees them. Doubtless thoughts will have passed through her mind that he met her when far from wife and home. At Haley's behest, Orfeon recorded Big Joe Turner with the Comets backing in late January 1966, the tracks being 'Low Down Dog', 'Flip, Flop And Fly', 'Monkey Man', 'Corrine, Corrina', 'Feeling Happy', 'Hide And Seek', 'Lonesome Train', 'Morning, Noon And Night', 'Honey Hush',and 'Stormy Monday Blues', issued on a single and two EPs. Haley then quit Orfeon in a dispute over royalty payments, the label issuing another two albums during the year, 'Whisky A Go Go' and 'Bill Haley A Go Go'. Spring 1966, and he is on a lengthy spell of military engagements in Germany when he receives an offer of a lucrative gig at Paris' Alambra Theatre, but sharing a bill with current English hit acts like the Spencer Davis Group and the Pretty Things. This was Britain 1964 again: Haley in incongruous company, a musical anachronism. From his perspective – and indeed from most R&R fans' perspective – the scene in '66 was even worse than '64. 1956 and rock'n'roll didn't seem like ten years ago – it felt more like fifty: for the scene had changed beyond recognition. Long-haired groups were everywhere, suits and manly attire were on the way out, gradually being replaced by the inexplicable and the bizarre; whilst musically, pop was becoming more pretentious, and 'meaningful' lyrics were coming into vogue. In a world of 20-year-old 'mod' culture – or whatever it was called in 1966 – the 41-year-old Haley had no idea where he and 'See You Later, Alligator' fitted in. Arriving in Paris, his morale was low and hit rock bottom when, emerging from his dressing room a girl remarked, 'What – are you still alive?'

Suffering the indignity of being the opening act for the new pop stars, the last thing he expected was: a thunderous applause, people waving 'Viva Bill Haley' banners and the place in uproar. Genuinely moved, Haley for once gave an extended set. The subsequent acts had to struggle through their sets to the relentless chant of 'Bill Haley! Bill Haley!' and for the second house it was agreed that they should open the show for him, he closing it! Spencer Davis reported to the *NME* that Haley was bigger than any of them and that he was a 'knock-out guy'.

Similar reactions occurred on subsequent dates in Ireland and Holland, the latter receiving newspaper headlines like, 'Bill Haley Brings Back Rock'n'Roll'. Haley must have been as much baffled as delighted. In point of fact what seemed to be happening is that the R&R fans of the Fifties were turning out in force in a reaction against the current pretentious music scene, yearning for the fun and spontaneity of Haley's music. Yet this 'underground' popularity was not translating into chart action – at least not for the present.

August 1967, and Haley recorded one of his best double-siders of the Sixties. It was another one-shot deal for a man who, alas, did not even have a label or the distribution to release it. He was the owner of a Phoenix night club Haley was playing and the record is of particular interest, for it was the *one and only time* he did a session without any Comets, not even Rudy Pompilii was present. Not in years had he shown such imagination and inventiveness and it really is criminal the record was never released. The two tracks could not have been more unlike, emphasising his interest in different markets. 'Jealous Heart', a country ballad hit of the '40s, which doubtless he often sang in those days, is set to a delicate arrangement by a Mexican trio with acoustic guitar and a gentle weeping steel guitar, whilst the singer's delivery carries a tender conviction. His pitch is perfect, conveying a heartache which avoids the bland sentimentality that characterised his early forays into this type of material. The startlingly different second side, 'Rock On, Baby', was written by the leader of a local 'rock' quartet Superfine Dandylion and was set to a chugging rhythm behind Haley's gruff delivery. Again, he revealed his remarkable vocal dexterity and not since 'I Got A Woman' had he sounded so different. This is the closest he ever got to a genuine contemporary 'rock' sound, a sound which some R&R fans, at least, could have got along with.

Haley is pigeon-holed as a failed hillbilly singer who found his niche in R&R, but beyond that he could not go. These sides, like some others, demonstrate what nonsense this perception is. Meanwhile, he was trapped in the R&R legend, which was not only his past and present, but also – as we shall see – his future. The winter of 1967/8, Haley, following a lengthy tour of Canada, got word of a burgeoning 'rock'n'roll revival' in Britain and that classic R&R records of the '50s were about to be reissued, including his 'Rock Around The Clock'. What the source of this revival was remains unclear, but it seemed to be a reaction against the 'flower power', protest songs and psychedelia of the day. MCA had acquired the Decca catalogue and began pushing Haley product, spearheaded by the release of 'Rock Around The Clock' in late January with 'Shake, Rattle And Roll' on the back. Airplay and sales were good and MCA may have had some role in his return to the UK in April, perfectly timed, as after some nine weeks, the record finally cracked *Record Retailer*'s Top 50. Also entering the chart the same week, was another MCA release, Buddy Holly's 'Peggy Sue'; and if that wasn't enough, EMI's reissue of Cochran's 'Summertime Blues' entered three weeks later. Holly would make No. 30, Cochran 34. *Record Retailer* put Haley as high as 20, but this – though it is considered the 'most authoritative' chart, is suspect, *NME*'s peak position of 28 being more realistic. Buoyed by these developments, Haley told *NME*, 'If Presley were on the next plane here, Jerry Lee Lewis, Little Richard and Fats Domino followed on another, we could Blitzkrieg England ... We could make it last five years. I am going to do my best ... but I can't do it on my own.' His gruelling five-week tour, taking in also Ireland, Sweden and Denmark, was a sell-out (11,000 saw him on two Scandinavian dates); some theatres, but mostly clubs, the biggest – and the one that made news – being London's Royal Albert Hall (May 1). It was packed and it seemed that every Teddy Boy and Girl in the country were there. The atmosphere was charged and volatile. Even opening R&R act Duane Eddy was almost in trouble for his new modern look and 'go go' dancers (which the audience just wanted to 'go'), only the Teddy Boy group, The Wild Angels, winning approval with their blast of several R&R classics. By the time the star appeared, the place was in uproar. Yet, for all the significance of the occasion – appearing at Britain's most prestigious venue and a record in the charts – he still only delivered the same standard 30-minute act, he singing, as Chris Gardner so aptly says, 'a handful of his greatest hits' and the Comets 'singing a handful of other people's hits'. When he closed his act with 'Rock Around The Clock' the stage was under siege and he and the Comets made a run for it. Stories of 'riots' and thuggery appeared in the following day's national press.

The Comets on this trip were the same quartet as '64, but for Johnny 'Bam Bam' Lane on drums. Nick Nastos played a twin-necked guitar which he later thought not a good idea for the back pain it gave him. Fans at Bristol had the unexpected treat of seeing Haley's young Mexican wife appear on stage to help her husband restring his guitar; his vigorous playing often leading to broken strings. The repertoire was little changed since '64, fans getting the Comets' versions of Chuck Berry and Little Richard hits when what they wanted to hear was Haley doing 'Hot Dog, Buddy, Buddy', '40 Cups Of Coffee' and so on. Not a chance. Apart from learning absolutely nothing from the UK in '57, what also dismayed those closely following his career was the contradiction between his public stance of spearheading the 'R&R revival' and the reality of his ambivalence towards it. He was at his hottest in years, 'Clock' remaining in the Top 50 'til the end of June, whilst climbing the German chart to No. 18 (with 'Summertime Blues' not far behind, reaching 25). It was also charting in Holland whilst in the States it was Top 40 in several regional markets, leading him to a return to lucrative TV appearances. Record companies were now *approaching him*, yet he vacillated. Here was the chance to rejuvenate his career with new records. R&R could only become a force again with new music: it would wither if seen only as retrogressive. So what does he do? Records an album of re-makes for the Swedish Sonet label, a project involving little preparation and rehearsal: quick money for minimal effort.

Bill Haley had more pressing things on his mind than any R&R revival. Back in the States, the Internal Revenue were trying to seize all his publishing copyrights; also booking contracts, so that promoters or club owners would be compelled to pay direct to it rather than to Haley. Moreover, his two ex-wives were hounding him for alimony.

Whilst yet in England, he played a US military venue to only 200 patrons – no 'R&R revival' there! Yet he gives them a 50-minute show, something he would not do for the Royal Albert Hall audience – estimated to be as much as 7000 – who idolised him and paid top dollar. How do you understand this man?

When he did record new material – in what seemed like a coup, for it was with United Artists, his first signing with a major since Decca and Warner – it would not be R&R at all, but a kind of easy listening country. Cut in New York (October 1968) with harmonica and an added string section, his rendering of 'That's How I Got To Memphis', a Tom T. Hall composition, is excellent; likewise the similar mood of the flip, 'Ain't Love Funny, Ha Ha'. It was his only single for the label (50483), but to our astonishment we learn that he turns down the label's offer of an album. Again we may surmise a tax reason for this. In any event, he was thinking short term and not long. Meanwhile, there were changes in the Comets: Al Rappa, tired of living out of a suitcase, quit after ten years, his place taken by Ray Cawley. Nick Nastos was replaced by Bill Miller, while the new drummer was the formidable Bill Nolte, who in addition to his thrilling percussion solos would also steal the show with his strong-voiced renderings of the country ballad hits of the day. He was easily the best Comets singer Haley ever had, Haley having the good sense to lift his 'ban' on ballads on stage to let him shine. Nolte and Cawley were two thirds of Nick Nastos and His Country Showmen which enjoyed a residency in a club backing visiting country stars. Though Nolte and Cawley were now also Comets, they officially remained in the employ of Nastos who paid them out of his cut of the fee paid to him by Pompilii. Nastos rejoined Haley for the singer's six-week tour of Scandinavia and England in summer 1969. The English trip could hardly have been more different to the last. During the last, he was the focus of media attention, he appeared on TV and radio, his Decca and Essex recordings were being reissued and even the films, 'Rock Around The Clock' and 'Don't Knock The Rock' were back on general release. On the charts, he was seen by some as the Messiah returning to overturn the detested new order and re-establish R&R forever. Some dream! A year was a long time in pop music back then: this time Haley played only northern venues and many were not even aware he was in the country. The 'rock'n'roll revival', as some of us suspected at the time, was a sham. Yet the music was not dead. An unexpected arrival amongst the hordes of long-haired groups was Credence Clearwater Revival with its summer 1969 smash, 'Bud Moon Rising', a record which sounded as if it could have been recorded in Memphis a decade earlier. In any event, the year closed on a high note for Haley with his triumphant appearance on Ralph Nader's 'Rock'n'Roll Revival' concerts. He had had grave misgivings about appearing, both Nader and Jolly Joyce having to spend many hours on the phone to persuade him, for he had not played a major venue in New York since probably 1958. A recording of one of these shows reveals an audience appreciative of the other acts (The Five Satins, Spaniels, etc.), but when Haley appears, the place erupts. Another positive development was the conclusion – at long last – of his troubles with the IRS. It is astonishing that these lasted as long as they did, since the fifties, but are indicative of his hopelessly shambolic financial affairs. It is also axiomatic that people who don't pay the tax man also don't pay others and we know that he was always in debt. He was still failing his alimony payments, and judgement by a court of law was filed against him. Despite his high earnings, he still overspent, sinking money into more doomed financial ventures. He was like King Midas in reverse: everything he touched turned to crap. He lived his life ducking and diving those to whom he owed, between holding up bars, inflicting his tales of bad luck on anyone within earshot. John Swenson's interview with Sam Charters, the singer's next producer, reveals a very depressing picture, hard to reconcile with the thoroughly like-able and homely public persona, of an impossibly dysfunctional and shambolic – and *rather nasty* – private man. Haley had been extremely lucky to have found a label like Sonet, whose owner Dag Heckses actually believed in him and his music. Heckses, who had since signed the singer to a three-year contract, was now about to indulge Haley in what he most wanted: to record a country album in Nashville. Meanwhile, 1970 had opened with another disappointing album, 'Bill Haley's Scrap Book' on Kama Sutra (KSB2014), which was yet another live recording of the stage act, another piece of easy money. A single from the LP was put out, 'Rock Around The Clock'/'Framed' (KS508), later reissued on Buddah (169).

9. Finale

Sonet producer Sam Charters had a challenge in Haley. Like Milt Gabler, he felt the singer's light, airy delivery was unsuitable for country. Haley wasn't happy with the material Charters presented, but he applied himself to it, working ceaselessly to adapt his delivery. But for all his effort, when the LP 'Rock Around The Country' (GP10040) was issued it met with a brick wall. It remains one of the great mysteries of the Haley story why he, so passionate about C&W, apart from that one time in 1952 with 'Icy Heart', should always be shunned by country radio. Inferior and less country sounding acts would get played, but never Haley. One of the LP's highlights, 'Me And Bobby McGee', the song itself much liked by country jocks, was considered to be the best version of his song by its writer, Kris Kristofferson. It seems that after the album, Haley returned to Mexico to concentrate on his mango growing business, about which he was in a feud with local cattle ranchers, and the building of a hotel. When not working as the Country Showmen, the Nastos trio went out on the road with Pompilii touring as 'Bill Haley's Comets', featuring Rudy Pompilii without Haley. 1971 passed and the new year brought rumours of Haley being very ill – his lungs blackened and his liver shot – but he re-emerged triumphant in 1972 performing in the internationally released R&R film documentary 'Let The Good Times Roll', which showed the shambolism of some 1955-61 acts, a foretaste of the Wembley Stadium R&R Concert in August, featuring Jerry Lee Lewis, Chuck Berry, Little Richard and Haley all on the same package, along with several others. It should have been the British R&R event of the century, but instead was almost a fiasco: far better one's memories of a decade earlier. Seeing this show made one realise that there could never be a serious revival. Perhaps by default, Bill Haley and His Comets came out as the show's real stars, in the view of not only R&R fans but also the pop press, perhaps because Haley delivered the same show with the same professionalism as he did in '57, unlike the others. This was all the more remarkable given his personal crisis.

Back in the studio in for a second Nashville album, 'Just Rock & Roll Music' (SNTF 645), Haley's drinking was observed as 'past the danger point'. Ominously, he was complaining of blinding headaches. He was so out of it he didn't even know where the microphone was. That the album got done at all was down to Sam Charter's patience and persistence, for just getting the singer into the studio was a feat. Haley managed to not only alienate everyone in Nashville – a place used to drunken musicians – but, worse still, he was alienating his own band. Unforgivably, he was not even paying Pompilii, without whom he could not perform, for he relied upon him for everything. He was both foul-mouthed and violent towards the Comets, all camaraderie had been shattered and they made it their business to avoid him as much as possible when not working. Only Pompilii would take the flak, day in day out. He felt sorry for Haley and always made excuses for him. Richard Nader, whose 'Rock'n'Roll Revival' shows were such a good source of income for Haley, got tired of his drinking and his unreliability and terminated his contract. There were tensions with Jolly Joyce, his long time booking agent and some time his US manager after Ferguson; and there are confused reports of tensions between Joyce and Paddy Malynn, his UK manager who had done so much for him in recent years. Secluded in his Veracruz ranch, this 'peaceable man' would take swipes at antagonists, and he was usually unreachable by phone, exasperating everyone north of the border. The BBC wanted him for a documentary about the development of pop music, someone telling them that 'Bill Haley is sick of being asked about rock'n'roll and is running a group of hotels in Mexico'. Charters was bewildered by the extent of Haley's confused personal and business affairs in which there was 'always some incredible catastrophe' happening.

But by the end of 1973, he flew out for his first tour of Australia since '57, and like then, that was quickly followed by a tour of Britain in February 1974 which would last some three months. Again he was to have the most extraordinary luck, due to circumstances outside his control. These circumstances again revolved around 'Rock Around The Clock', the hit that refused to go away. The record was chosen as the theme of the new hit TV sitcom series, 'Happy Days' and would be heard week in, week out by millions of a new generation; and then it was the thrilling intro to George Lucas' surprise hit film, 'American Graffiti', its soundtrack going into the US LP charts. MCA meanwhile made a concerted transatlantic push on the single and on March 16 it entered the UK Top Fifty. The tour was a great success, many venues being complete sell-outs, but at the Hammersmith Palais (March 25) in West London the management sold 1000 tickets over the 3000 capacity, creating tensions within the hall. The show was recorded for an LP, 'Live In London' and was a longer set than usual, but Haley's refusal to give an encore led to a riot, reported in the following day's papers. However, Haley had to leave quickly, for he was already booked into another venue in nearby Kensington on the same night. The previous week he had played seven nights at sell-out clubs in Oldham and Brighouse and was an honorary guest of Leeds United football club on the 23rd, taking front row seats in the Director's box at Elland Road. It must have been an event for Haley, for he had never seen an English football league game before, the team playing against Burnley. At half time it was announced to fans that Bill Haley was the club's guest and his records were played. What an occasion! According to Trevor Simpson (*Now Dig This*, 254), the source for this report, Haley's wife was with him on this tour. At this time, he had visibly aged – 48, but looking 68 – his face ravaged. Sometimes his face looked puffed, other times oddly gaunt. One peculiarity, on some dates, was his kiss curl placed on the opposite side above his bad eye. The Comets on this tour were, apart from Pompilii and Nastos, Ray Cawley, bass, Ray Parsons, rhythm, and Freddy Moore, drums. For once they didn't wear jacket and tie, but a brightly coloured kind of vest – waistcoat – which fortunately they would not wear again.

Haley's profile was strong again as 'Rock Around The Clock' rose to No. 12 in *Record Retailer*'s chart and 13 in the *NME*. He appeared on various radio and TV shows, even on 'Top Of The Pops', and most unusually for Haley, he alluded to his drink problem in one interview. Moreover, 'Rock Around The Clock' was now also climbing the US charts, his biggest success there since 1958: it would reach No. 36 in *Cash Box*, whose Top 100 was based solely on sales, and 39 in *Billboard* whose Hot 100 was split between sales and airplay. From this we can deduce that just like in 1955, for all the changes in the record business in the intervening period, Haley's sales always outstripped airplay.

The American hit led to a highly successful tour of the West Coast, followed by a tour of the East. It was at this time Haley fell out with Jolly Joyce to whom he was still contracted for personal appearances. He had long suspected that Joyce was ripping him off, a suspicion confirmed when he saw his fee shoot up when another agent booked his East Coast tour. But Haley was in violation of his contract and this would have serious consequences. November and December saw another successful European tour, but several of the band returned home ill. Pompilii and lead guitarist Bill Turner took to their beds. Pompilii was down with pneumonia, spending Christmas and New Year in hospital. The saxophonist had been unwell for some time, given to bouts of coughing prompted by a 'knotted feeling' in his chest. Hospital tests revealed a more sinister development: a tumour on his lung. That this was cancer was not known to all until March 1975 when the Comets travelled to Nashville for not one but two Sonet albums, Haley's next, and a project that had been planned for some time, Pompilii's own album featuring Haley and the Comets as sidemen. A shadow hung over the enterprise, for this was the seventies and if one had cancer death was almost certainly in the offing. Astonishingly, Haley, instead of taking a plane, opted to drive up from Veracruz to Nashville: which is like driving from London to Athens for a recording session instead of taking a plane. It may be that Haley had other business to attend to en route, but it seems his only ports of call along the way were bars and by the time he reached Texas he was three days late, stone drunk and his car broke down. His brothers-in-law drove up to bring him back. Sam Charters pitied Pompilii and the band waiting around in their motel for days, only to have to pack up and return home. Even now Pompilii made excuses for Haley. A few months later, Charters sought to save the saxophonist's aborted album. To save him the travelling, the producer went to Pennsylvania and rented a local studio, using local musicians as the Comets were unavailable. Charters got the album done, but at a price. Given his ailing condition, Pompilii turned out a remarkable performance, but was failed by the undistinguished sidemen. Meanwhile, with Haley sloshed in Mexico, Pompilii continued his local act, called Rudy Pell and The Happy Days – presumably a cash-in on the TV show. It is often asked why this supremely gifted musician abandoned a promising career in jazz in the mid-'50s to join a controversial R&R act. There is no mystery to this, for despite his gentle nature, he was a born showman. He couldn't help it: he was born to tear the house down – and you couldn't do that in jazz! Staggeringly, in late '75, seriously ill and in great pain he performed his sensational act at the Nite Cap lounge, leaping on to the bar, never spilling a drink, snake dancing through the crowd which followed him around the room and out into the parking lot!

Hospital bills, medication and the horrendous cost of chemo-therapy (causing him now to wear a wig) had devoured Pompilii's finances: Haley offered to help, but 'offer' is all he did. The only work he had for him and the Comets for the whole year was a tour of Brazil in October. We may be surprised that Pompilii didn't tell Haley to take a walk. Maybe because he needed the money; but he couldn't shake off his loyalty to his 'friend' and employer. Haley always had a charming way about him and Pompilii was always kind-hearted and forgiving. But there were those who thought that deep down he probably resented Haley. He tried to be a good Catholic, but he wasn't a saint; Apart from a brief marriage in the 1940s, he had been a life-long bachelor, but in November 1975 he married Anne Scott. February 5, 1976, he died and was buried on the 9th. There was a great turnout at his funeral for one of Chester's most popular and best-loved musicians. Family, friends, Comets past and present were there. But no Bill Haley.

Haley was lost without Pompilii. His closest friend – whom he referred to as his 'brother' – had done everything. He took care of every aspect of the band, he kept a ledger of income and expenditure, he checked royalty statements, and so on. All Haley had to do was show up. Haley supposedly went into 'retirement' after Pompilii's death, in respect of his memory. He would tell reporters a touching story of how he and his best friend had a kind of 'pact': if one predeceased the other, the survivor would not perform again. But in point of fact Haley had not been working regularly anyway and no sooner had Pompilii died than he was hit by a massive lawsuit by booking agent Sandra Shekell whom had acquired Haley's contract from the Joyce agency; moreover Haley was stopped from performing anywhere in the US. Unhappily posthumous, Pompilii's album, 'The Sax That Changed The World!!' was issued in Britain only to limited sales. Remarkably, the sales on Haley's first two Sonet albums had combined sales of over half a million, testifying to his enduring European popularity. Bill Turner had organised a new set of Comets for Haley's return to Europe in the Spring, but at the last moment the singer cancelled, which may have incurred more litigation. Next, Haley was back in the studio with Sam Charters, but this time at Muscle Shoals. Haley seemed to be off the juice, but the sessions were tinged with sadness. With his sax player and confidant gone, Haley was both deflated and rudderless. Whilst he used to refer to him as his 'brother' in truth Pompilii was more like a father, notwithstanding that they were both of similar age, constantly supporting, encouraging and guiding him at every twist and turn. Whilst Haley was the focus of the act, Pompilii was its heart. The heart gone, Haley felt alone and directionless. Charters' problem was finding new material for Haley. Ideally, in the mid-'70s Haley should have developed as a country act, following the route of other rockers like Jerry Lee Lewis and Conway Twitty, but their voices were ideal for the medium whilst Haley's was problematic. So given his European popularity, it was better to stick to R&R, but nobody in the US was writing R&R, so no new material was available. What is so odd is why Haley, a highly gifted and prolific songwriter in the '50s, was not writing new material himself; even stranger, given his past obsession with owning the songs he recorded. As Charters observed, Haley could not be given 'sexy' songs: he was identified with non-erotic happy nonsensical music of which he was master. So the outcome of this latest album (to be called 'R-O-C-K'; Sonet SNTF700) was another set of re-makes of his Decca and Essex past. The only 'new' song, as far as Haley was concerned, was a version of the Charlie Rich hit, 'Mohair Sam', the only number on which he and the Muscle Shoals sessionmen could gel, for they, of a new generation, did not understand R&R. That was the other problem recording Haley: his approach was rooted in the 50s whilst he had to work with musicians trained in the gutless contemporary style. Which begs the question why were Sonet recording in the US where no-one understood R&R and not in Britain – its spiritual home – where a whole new generation of musicians, particularly Teddy Boy groups like Shakin' Stevens and The Sunsets, Crazy Cavan and The Rhythm Rockers and The Flying Saucers – were in the ascendant. With any of them Haley would have gelled. Stuff Nashville or Muscle Schoals: a far better place would have been South Wales: producer Paul Barrett, the band Rockin' Louie and The Mama Jammers; the result – dynamite!

1976 closed on an uneasy note. December 1, Jack Howard died in Philadelphia, another support gone. Back in England, Teddy Boy hooliganism marred Haley's performance at London's Victoria Theatre, leading to injuries and arrests. Haley came with a new line-up of Comets who did the job they were paid to do, but did not, unlike Bill Turner, actually understand Haley's legacy or musical ethos, nor had much reason to, for off stage the singer remained aloof. 'The trouble with Haley', said one, 'is that he thinks he's a big star.' Then in the States, the Sandra Shekell lawsuit left him with almost a quarter of a million dollars to pay in damages – equating to many millions in today's values. Here, another mystery appears. How on earth did he pay this when in 1971 he stopped performing altogether? He shut himself away in Veracruz, refusing all contact with the music world. He later told reporters he had 'gone into hiding', an unfortunate phrase given his reputation, because he 'missed Rudy'. About Mexico he said, 'It's a place to get away from it all. Man, down here ... they don't know from nothin' or care ... It's a home. It's not a big deal. I'm a very conservative guy, not one of those millionaires. I'm not a Presley-type guy.' But surely he was not so naive as to think that escaping to Mexico he could escape Shekell's curse. This period is clouded in obscurity and contradiction, and how Haley, a man who always lived on the edge financially, coped with such a massive financial liability is not explained. It is almost certain that at this time he had extensive surgery on a brain tumour, another big financial liability. His only income presumably was from song and record royalties which could never be enough to meet his needs. He was – or had been – operating a fishing boat charter business in addition to growing mangos and building a hotel, but these ventures were attended by 'catastrophes' (Charters), so it is doubtful if they augmented his income (probably the contrary).

After more than two years in obscurity he reappeared in Britain, not once but twice in 1979, with yet another set of Comets, some now being British, presumably organised by Mal Gray, who also went on tour performing solo singing spots as a kind of honorary Comet. Again we may remark at how well received Haley is in England, the year's highlight for him being his appearance at the Royal Command Performance in the presence of the Queen and watched by millions on TV. He does two verses of 'See You Later, Alligator' and then into 'Rock Around The Clock'. The Queen was apparently a fan in 1956 and the Palace probably owned copies of the records; but we would be more impressed if we knew it also had copies of 'Be Bop A Lula' and 'Long Tall Sally'! After the show, he was lined up with a host of other stage and film stars to shake hands with the Queen, Haley beaming from ear to ear like a bashful schoolboy. Unconnected to this occasion was his appearance at the Royalty Ballroom at Southgate in North London, captured on film for the Teddy Boy documentary, 'Blue Suede Shoes'. The film is a remarkable testament to the Haley phenomenon. The venue is packed tight with Teds and other youths. Gone are the days when one could expect to see Bill Haley and *The* Comets, the audience knowing it was just another makeshift crew; they are only there to see him. When he walks on, they go wild. At 53, he is probably twice to three times the age of his audience, his face puffed, eyes almost closed, he's perspiring. Yet no one could know that he was a very ill man. The voice is exactly the same as in 1955 and he belts out each number with the same gusto as though a quarter of a century had never passed. And again we witness the same gentlemanly manner which sets him apart from the norm. What is so extraordinary is that, despite the musical upheavals of the decades, *with the Haley phenomenon nothing has changed*. Here he is in 1979 playing to people half his age, exactly the way it was in 1954! There is something strangely fascinating and heartwarming about this, for youth culture demands youth idols; but Haley at all times was old enough to be his audience's father. And when he breaks into 'Rock Around The Clock' the audience erupts into a frenzy, even though many – if not most – weren't even born in 1955!

All R&R fans go wild when their heroes do their 'big number', Lewis' 'Whole Lotta Shakin'', Perkins' 'Blue Suede Shoes', and so on, but when Haley did 'Clock' it was always pandemonium. Why? What was this extraordinary effect – which even thrilled the nervous Haley – every time he broke into this song? Apart from the fact that it is the song that ignited the rock'n'roll explosion, I cannot explain it. But, as we know, Haley always failed his audiences by never delivering enough and often palpably without conviction – yet they kept coming back. Is it because they recognised that he was the only *genuine* original rocker left? Because when Haley walked on, he gave exactly the same performance he gave in '55, '56 and '57; which could not be said of the other original rockers. Moreover, he always, unfailingly, attired himself in jacket and stage tie, a continuity of the '50s, unlike the others who abandoned any dress connection with the era. Haley never tried to be anything but himself: he didn't try to be an 18-year-old, audiences accepting him for what he was. Those who rubbish Haley for not being sexy or wild can eat their hearts out: it wasn't necessary, for the crowds went wild the moment he walked on. Few others had such an effect.

Late June 1979 he had been back at Muscle Shoals, this time with English producer Kenny Denton. The album 'Everybody Can Rock'n'Roll' (SNTF 808) did at least have three new R&R songs, including the title track. Haley's wife Maria and their 15-year old son were present and in a tape of the session rehearsals subsequently published by Denton we hear a likeable and focused Bill Haley at work, far removed from the cantankerous drunk we've heard of late. Photos from the sessions show a happy scene of Haley and family, producer and musicians. Denton had nothing but good to say of Haley. But sadly by the time he was next in Europe something was seriously wrong. He did several continental TV appearances including one in which his *two front teeth* were missing! Yet his delivery was unimpaired. But much more ominously, and totally out of character, were bizarre reports of undressing on stage. Such bizarre behaviour was not denied by Patrick Malynn, who had since learnt that the singer's brain tumour had become inoperable.

May and June 1980 saw his last overseas tour in South Africa. It is thought to be Haley's last appearance anywhere. Divorce was again in the air, he now becoming the ex-husband of three wives and the father of three families. He moved to Harlingen in Texas, just inside the Mexican border, where he began to drink himself to death. He would telephone his ex-wives in the early hours of the morning with incoherent monologues, rather than conversations, which would ramble on for an hour. They put up with it out of pity; they will have known his days were numbered. These phone calls were innocuous enough, unlike the nocturnal calls to business associates such as Rex Zario who worked for Essex in the old days and took over Haley's publishing interests after Jack Howard's death in '76. These were nasty and senseless and, in a transcript of one of them published by Zario, it is hard to escape the conclusion that Haley was clinically insane. It may be his obsessive paranoia which made him make calls in the middle of the night – perhaps the product of a lifetime ducking and diving pursuing creditors and ex-wives – he perhaps thinking that at that hour 'they' would not be listening in. He moved out of his house into the garage thinking 'they' wouldn't find him there. He was found wandering on lonely country roads, confused and lost. In restaurants he would order meals but not eat them, staring into space. He would approach other patrons telling them that he was 'Bill Haley' of 'Rock Around The Clock' fame, 'but don't tell anyone'.

February 9, 1981, five years to the day of Rudy Pompilii's funeral, Bill Haley suffered a fatal heart attack, apparently in his sleep.

About the time of his death there was talk of a Hollywood biography starring Jeff Bridges – but 'talk' is all it remained. By summer 1981 there was a 'Bill Haley's Comets' on the scene, the group's only claim to authenticity being lead guitarist Franny Beecher. By 1987 there were no less than three different 'Bill Haley's Comets' on tour, none featuring the original members. At last, in the same year, New York lawyer and Haley devotee, David Hirschberg, accomplished what the singer himself had failed to do – reform the original Comets: Johnny Grande, Marshall Lytle, Joey Ambrose, Dick Richards and Franny Beecher; joined temporarily by Bill Turner, Haley's lead guitarist, 1974-77.

In Britain, Haley's memory lived on through acts such as The Stargazers, Jackie Buddin and the fabulous Lucas & The Dynamos, and from Germany, Bill Haley's Revival Band. More recent years have seen the appearance of 'tribute' acts such as Phil Haley & His Comments (!) and Razzle Dazzle. The ensuing decades have seen any number of Haley anthologies on vinyl and CD, the cream of which have been Bear Family's superlative box sets and Hydra's compilations of rare live material. Hydra's owner, Klaus Kettner, in 2006 opened a museum in Munich dedicated to his hero, displaying a mouth-watering array of Haleyana.

It is worthy of note that the reformed Comets have lasted far longer than they ever did originally! Perhaps not such a great compliment to their missing leader. One highlight of their long reunion was the occasion of July 5/6, 2005, when they performed a series of shows commemorating half a century to the week since 'Rock Around The Clock' made No. 1 and what would have been Bill Haley's 80th birthday. A day earlier, 83 million miles into space, NASA's Deep Impact probe had successfully crashed a comet. Comets manager, Martin Lewis, had earlier promised that, if the mission was successful, his act would perform for the NASA staff without charge. Amongst the audience was one Maggie Porter, whom in 1957 was on Haley's train to Waterloo and had his name tattooed on her arm! 'Everyone was getting Bill Haley tattoos,' she said. It cost her half a crown (25p) and a smacking from her mother! Present at these shows were Joan 'Cuppy' Haley – looking radiant and youthful in a photo by Alex Fraser-Harrison, the source of this report – and Peter Ford and Gina Haley, child of her father's third marriage, and a songwriter and singer in her own right. She was flabbergasted when, in a show on the occasion of the bronze engraving of Haley and the Comets' names on Hollywood's Rockwalk, she was called to come up to the stage to sing with her Dad's group. So that was the night Gina Haley and The Comets gave out with 'Rock The Joint' and 'Rock Around The Clock'. These events received extensive coverage from the media which was astonished by the rock'n'rollin' energy of a group whose eldest members were in their eighties. When all was over, everyone gathered in the tour bus singing 'Happy Birthday' for the man whom, despite everything, they still loved.

INDEX

95

100